"When we began reading *Life with Sophie*, it was at a time in our lives when my daughter was facing some of the same scenarios presented in the book. She could relate to Sophie and learn how to consider her responses and actions from a biblical perspective by the scenarios, questions and applicable verses presented with each devotional. This is what Evie had to say: 'I really like it a lot! It was the best book ever!'"

—Ruth Robins,

Norfolk, Virginia

"The chapter entitled 'A Trusting Heart' helped my son as that had been a specific area where he struggled. It made sense to him and was helpful in using it as an object lesson. As a boy, he was really fascinated with 'The Deep and Terrible Woods,' and his favorite project was the 'name poster,' which gave a foundation for his name having great meaning."

—April Truit,

Franklin, VA

"*Life with Sophie* is a great tool to equip parents in dealing with difficult issues in a Biblical way. The hands on activities of each chapter along with the scripture memory verses were unique ways to demonstrate and engrave God's word on our child's heart. It is a great resource to help parents guide their children in the way of wisdom."

—Marien Gomez,

Suffolk, Va.

"The book has been so much fun. I've never seen Aisha so excited about devotion. For the activity in celebrating friends, she spent days making handcrafted cards and writing in them a sweet message. 'Jazelle's Story' was a great forgiveness lesson and I also like the introduction to salvation with kids. I realized you need to talk about it often to know if they really understand salvation."

—Kinya Karmi,

Africa

"*Life with Sophie* is a great resource for parents to use with their children. The story, activities, devotionals, and questions provide opportunities for parents and their children to interact together. I would highly recommend using this in your family."

—Brett Carl

Pastor of Missions, Westminster Reformed Presbyterian Church,

Suffolk, VA

Life with
Sophie

Life with Sophie
learning the pathway of wisdom

Shirley Porter

Life with Sophie

Trilogy Christian Publishers A Wholly Owned Subsidiary of Trinity Broadcasting Network

2442 Michelle Drive, Tustin, CA 92780

Copyright © 2023 by Shirley Porter

Scripture quotations marked ESV are taken from the ESV® Bible (The Holy Bible, English Standard Version®), copyright © 2001 by Crossway Bibles, a publishing ministry of Good News Publishers. Used by permission. All rights reserved. Scripture quotations marked NASB are taken from the New American Standard Bible® (NASB), Copyright © 1960, 1962, 1963, 1968, 1971, 1972, 1973, 1975, 1977, 1995 by The Lockman Foundation. Used by permission. www.Lockman.org. Scripture quotations marked NIV are taken from the Holy Bible, New International Version®, NIV®. Copyright © 1973, 1978, 1984, 2011 by Biblica, Inc.TM Used by permission of Zondervan. All rights reserved worldwide. www.zondervan.com. The "NIV" and "New International Version" are trademarks registered in the United States Patent and Trademark Office by Biblica, Inc.TM Scripture quotations marked NLT are taken from the Holy Bible, New Living Translation, copyright © 1996, 2004, 2015 by Tyndale House Foundation. Used by permission of Tyndale House Publishers, Inc., Carol Stream, Illinois 60188. All rights reserved.

No part of this book may be reproduced, stored in a retrieval system, or transmitted by any means without written permission from the author. All rights reserved. Printed in the USA.

Rights Department, 2442 Michelle Drive, Tustin, CA 92780.

Trilogy Christian Publishing/TBN and colophon are trademarks of Trinity Broadcasting Network.

For information about special discounts for bulk purchases, please contact Trilogy Christian Publishing.

Trilogy Disclaimer: The views and content expressed in this book are those of the author and may not necessarily reflect the views and doctrine of Trilogy Christian Publishing or the Trinity Broadcasting Network.

Manufactured in the United States of America

10 9 8 7 6 5 4 3 2 1

Library of Congress Cataloging-in-Publication Data is available.

ISBN: 979-8-88738-139-8

E-ISBN: 979-8-88738-140-4

Dedication

To Tom—my husband, my love, my best friend.

Preface

Several years ago, I started a study on the Book of Proverbs. Having been a believer for many years, I had done many studies in the Bible, studies of different books in the Old Testament and the New Testament, and I had certainly read the Proverbs but had never studied it in any depth. Yet when I started the study of this wonderful book, I realized more and more that it was filled with wonderful stories that could help parents give children assuring and practical ways of living everyday life. And this would result in implanting the desire for wisdom, God's wisdom. I grieved that I did not understand these lessons when my children were young. I would often stop and pray, "Oh, Father, I wish there was a way to teach this very abstract quality called wisdom to children." During this time, while attending a class on the gifts of the Spirit, I was asked by our leader, Nan Olson, one of the godliest women I have ever known and who is now rejoicing in heaven, to give a lesson on the gift of wisdom. When I researched the word, I found the word wisdom comes from the Greek word *Sophia*, and one morning shortly after, I awoke with this thought, *What if there was a little girl named Sophie who wondered and wondered about her name?* And *Life with Sophie* was born.

Thus, while Sophie is often the "heroine" of each chapter, you will find that her life is filled with family and friends who all become "parts" of the story. Stories of wonderful times and sometimes stories of great sadness. They are written as a springboard for parents (single parents, adoptive parents, or parents with birth mom and dad) to introduce and teach this very abstract quality of wisdom which is rooted in the Book of Proverbs. It is a quality described in Proverbs 9:10 (NIV) as "The fear of the Lord is the beginning of wisdom, and the knowledge of the Holy One is understanding."

When we look at the way Jesus taught, we read in the Gospel of Mark

4:33–34 (NIV), "With many similar parables Jesus spoke the word to them, as much as they could understand. He did not say anything to them without using a parable. But when He was alone with His disciples, He explained everything." I have tried to follow this example in each chapter with the story and devotionals. And I have endeavored to write "parables" of adventures and mishaps where Sophie and her friends get involved. Each "story" lesson and devotional comes with a "Parent's Guide" with suggestions and activities. The parents contribute to the stories in such a way as to plant seeds of truth, trust, and understanding. It is an understanding not only of how deeply their children are loved but also that Jesus is always interested in what happens in their everyday lives and will be with them in every step they take and every lesson learned. If there are older teenagers, they can help enormously in reading the stories or helping with the activities and thereby learn the blessings of becoming mentors to their sisters or brothers.

My prayer is that this book will support the proclamation by Moses to his people from Deuteronomy 6:6–7 (NIV), "These commandments that I give you today are to be on your hearts. Impress them on your children. Talk about them when you sit at home and when you walk along the road, when you lie down and when you get up."

I hope you will enjoy Sophie, her family, her wonderful friend Jackson (who is also her cousin), and this story of a little girl who just loves life and wonders about so many, many things.

Prayerfully,
Shirley Porter

Acknowledgments

How do you say "thank you" to so many who have been instrumental in the process of this "offering"? To Tom, my husband, who has stood by me, prayed consistently for me, listened to my frustrations, and constantly pointed me to Jesus. To our daughter, Cyndi, who has faithfully prayed and given good suggestions and so many times has set aside her schedule to help me. To Roxanne Clark, who made the book presentable with her expert editing of the first draft. To the couples in our Bible study group who meet every Thursday evening and have continued to pray and encourage me. To the moms and dads who have done the study with their children and given such helpful reviews. And to the children who loved Sophie (what a blessing you have been to me). And last but certainly not least, to Bonnie Horne, our photographer, who prayerfully and so diligently gave of her time and wonderful abilities in photography. And to my wonderful "sister friends," Debi Gick and Diane Nelms, who willingly made special trips to my home to help me with the word processing elements of editing. Without their expertise in computer knowledge of program after program, their prayerful advice, encouragement, and suggestions, I truly may have never had the book ready to put into book form. "Thank you" all. You have blessed me abundantly!

Parent's Guide

Welcome to the joy of Proverbs, its wisdom, and its wonders. At the beginning of each chapter, you will find a "Parent's Guide" that will give you the emphasis of the chapter, a family activity, the memory verse for the week, and suggested answers for the "What Do You Think?" questions.

There are ten chapters, and each chapter (ideally) would be read on a Monday by a parent or older sibling. The longest chapter is 8–10 minutes. The family activity can follow the reading of the chapter, or it can be done the next day (Tuesday). There are three devotionals which are 3 or 4 minutes and can easily be done at the breakfast table, at the evening meal, or (preferably) at bedtime. These devotionals would then be done on Wednesday, Thursday, and Friday.

The devotionals have purposely been written to be not more than 3–4 minutes, and the activities, with the exception of two or three, require little advance preparation and are easily done. We all realize how difficult (life's) schedules are (mom's and dad's and children's school schedules with sports, music lessons, etc.). And while the devotionals are based on scriptural principles that our children need to know, and most of the activities require little preparation, it is (as Moses of old requested) the "talking about God's principles when you sit at home" (at the breakfast or dinner table) and when you "walk along the road" (or doing a simple activity), and when you "lie down" (conversation and prayer before bedtime) that allows parents to connect with their children on a daily basis. And as you cover them in prayer, they will, by your actions and time with them, always remember how "fun" their Lord is, how "big and mighty" their God is, and how the Holy Spirit is with them every day and hour of their lives, and they will be able when they are older to look back and treasure the daily lessons and impressions of a family rooted in our Lord's magnificent Word.

"These commandments that I give you today are to be on our hearts. Impress them on your children. Talk about them when you sit at home and when you walk along the road, when you lie down and when you get up" (Deuteronomy 6:6–7, NIV).

Table of Contents

CHAPTER 1: I Wonder—What Is Wisdom? 21

Parent's Guide for Chapter 1:I Wonder—What Is Wisdom? 22

Chapter One:I Wonder—What Is Wisdom? 25

Supply List for Activity 1 32

Parent's Guide for Chapter 1 Devotional 1:The Wisdom of Solomon 34

Chapter 1 Devotional 1:The Wisdom of Solomon 36

Parent's Guide for Chapter 1 Devotional 2:What Is Fear of the Lord? 40

Chapter 1 Devotional 2:What Is Fear of the Lord? 42

Parent's Guide for Chapter 1 Devotional 3:What Comes after *the Beginning*? 45

Chapter 1 Devotional 3:What Comes after *the Beginning?* *48*

CHAPTER 2:Treasuring a Good Name. 51

Parent's Guide for Chapter 2:Treasuring a Good Name 52

Chapter Two:Treasuring a Good Name 55

Supply List for Activity 2 62

Parent's Guide for Chapter 2 Devotional 1:What Does God's Name

Mean? 63

Chapter 2 Devotional 1: What Does God's Name Mean? 66

Parent's Guide for Chapter 2 Devotional 2: What's in a Name? .. 69

Chapter 2 Devotional 2: What's in a Name? 70

Parent's Guide for Chapter 2 Devotional 3: The Old Pictures 75

Chapter 2 Devotional 3: The Old Pictures 77

CHAPTER 3: A Trusting Heart 81

Parent's Guide for Chapter 3: A Trusting Heart 82

Chapter Three: A Trusting Heart 85

Supply List for Activity 3 91

Parent's Guide for Chapter 3 Devotional 1: Trusting in the Lord . 93

Chapter 3 Devotional 1: Trusting in the Lord 95

Parent's Guide for Chapter 3 Devotional 2: United Attention ... 99

Chapter 3 Devotional 2: United Attention 101

Parent's Guide for Chapter 3 Devotional 3: Elizabeth's Friend .. 104

Chapter 3 Devotional 3: Elizabeth's Friend 106

CHAPTER 4: Sophie Speaks about Good Friends 109

Parent's Guide for Chapter 4: Sophie Speaks about
Good Friends 110

Chapter Four: Sophie Speaks about Good Friends 113

Supply List for Activity 4 118

Parent's Guide for Chapter 4 Devotional 1: What Is a
Good Friend? 121

Chapter 4 Devotional 1: What Is a Good Friend? 123

Parent's Guide for Chapter 4 Devotional 2: Sophie's
New Friend 126

Chapter 4 Devotional 2: Sophie's New Friend 128

Parent's Guide for Chapter 4 Devotional 2: Sophie's
New Friend 131

Chapter 4 Devotional 3: Listening to Good Advice 133

CHAPTER 5: The Deep and Terrible Woods **137**

Parent's Guide for Chapter 5: The *Deep* and *Terrible* Woods—
Disobedience 138

Chapter Five: The *Deep* and *Terrible* Woods—Disobedience 141

Supply List for Activity 5 147

Roleplay 1: Skateboarding 148

Roleplay 2: Looking Stylish 150

Roleplay 3: "But Everyone Does It!" 152

Parent's Guide for Chapter 5 Devotional 1: Elizabeth's Story . . . 154

Chapter 5 Devotional 1: Elizabeth's Story 156

Parent's Guide for Chapter 5 Devotional 2: Let the Children
Come to Me 160

Chapter 5 Devotional 2:Let the Children Come to Me 162

Parent's Guide for Chapter 5 Devotional 3:Samson and Delilah 165

Chapter 5 Devotional 3:Samson and Delilah 167

CHAPTER 6:The Deep and Terrible Trouble **171**

Parent's Guide for Chapter 6:The *Deep* and *Terrible* Trouble—
Consequences 172

Chapter Six:The *Deep* and *Terrible* Trouble—Consequences. . . . 175

Supply List for Activity 6 182

Parent's Guide for Chapter 6 Devotional 1:Doing the Right
Thing. 184

Chapter 6 Devotional 1:Doing the Right Thing 185

Parent's Guide for Chapter 6 Devotional 2:A Lesson Learned! . 189

Chapter 6 Devotional 2:A Lesson Learned! 191

Parent's Guide for Chapter 6 Devotional 3:Wisdom from Aunt
Kikky. 194

Chapter 6 Devotional 3:Wisdom from Aunt Kikky 196

CHAPTER 7:Lies and Ugly Words. **201**

Parent's Guide for Chapter 7:Lies and Ugly Words 202

Chapter Seven:Lies and Ugly Words 205

Supply List for Activity 7 212

Parent's Guide for Chapter 7 Devotional 1:Losing Trust 215

Chapter 7 Devotional 1:Losing Trust 217

Parent's Guide for Chapter 7 Devotional 2:Aunt Kikky's Story .220

Chapter 7 Devotional 2:Aunt Kikky's Story 222

Parent's Guide for Chapter 7 Devotional 3:Growing Up 226

Chapter 7 Devotional 3:Growing Up .228

CHAPTER 8:Forgiveness and Grace 233

Parent's Guide for Chapter 8:Forgiveness and Grace 234

Chapter Eight:Forgiveness and Grace. 237

Supply List for Activity 8 244

Parent's Guide for Chapter 8 Devotional 1:Remember When? .246

Chapter 8 Devotional 1:Remember When? 249

Parent's Guide for Chapter 8 Devotional 2:My Bike
Was Stolen! 253

Chapter 8 Devotional 2:My Bike Was Stolen!* 255

Parent's Guide for Chapter 8 Devotional 3:Who Is the Prodigal
Son? 258

Chapter 8 Devotional 3:Who Is the Prodigal Son? 260

CHAPTER 9:A Shelter in the Storm 265

Parent's Guide for Chapter 9:A Shelter in the Storm 266

Chapter Nine:A Shelter in the Storm .269

Supply List for Activity 9 277

Parent's Guide for Chapter 9 Devotional 1:A Good Day! 280

Chapter 9 Devotional 1:A Good Day! .281

Parent's Guide for Chapter 9 Devotional 2:Completing
a Mission. 286

Chapter 9 Devotional 2:Completing a Mission 288

Parent's Guide for Chapter 9 Devotional 3:Shining Answers...
Like the Morning Sun! 293

Chapter 9 Devotional 3:Shining Answers...Like the Morning
Sun!. 295

CHAPTER 10:Sophie's Dream 299

Parent's Guide for Chapter 10:Sophie's Dream. 300

Chapter Ten:Sophie's Dream 303

Supply List for Activity 10 308

Activity 10:Apples of Wisdom 308

Chapter Reminders. 309

Instructions for the Wisdom of Apples Tree. 312

Endnotes 317

CHAPTER 1:

I Wonder—What Is Wisdom?

Parent's Guide for Chapter 1: I Wonder—What Is Wisdom?

Emphasis

The wonder of wisdom. To wonder is to be very curious or astonished about things we see or hear. And Sophie wonders about so many things. It can be huge, like the vastness of a mighty waterfall, or it can be really simple, like, "Why doesn't my sister like chocolate ice cream?" But in this first chapter, Sophie wonders about her name and finds out from her mom that it comes from the Greek word *Sophia*, which in English is translated as "wisdom." Her mom shares her desire for Sophie to see where wisdom starts and how it can be used in all that she learns as she grows up. The following verse introduces the theme of the book.

Memory Verse: "The fear of the Lord is the beginning of wisdom, and knowledge of the Holy One is understanding" (Proverbs 9:10, NIV).

Sophie's mom tries to help her see how the magnificence and magnitude of God produces a reverent and awesome "holy fear."

Suggested Answers to "What Do You Think?" Questions

1. Tell me the first thing that comes into your mind when I say the following words: God, Jesus, Holy Spirit.

   You want their instant response to each of these words. It will help you get an understanding of the way they perceive God.

2. Why do you think Sophie was asking about wisdom?

   Her mom told her that the name Sophie means "wisdom," and she wanted to know what that meant.

3. Who needs wisdom? Why?

   We all need the wisdom that comes from God so that each of us can understand what "truth" is. God tells us to search for wisdom as we would search for a great treasure.

4. Would you like to know what your name means?

   Keep reading because that is exactly what you will find out in the next chapter.

Chapter One:
I Wonder—What Is Wisdom?

In a lovely country and in a lovely town, there lived a little girl named Sophie who was ten years old and who wondered about many, many things. To wonder, you know, means to be amazed or really curious about something. And Sophie had a lot of those "wonders." She wondered why it was that, especially after it rained all night, she would hear the birds singing early in the morning. She wondered why there were five days of school and only two days off. And why did God make 24 hours in a day instead of 20? She wondered about the colors of flowers; she wondered why so many adults had that little wrinkle in their faces right between their eyes; she wondered why her big sister didn't like chocolate ice cream and why little puppies made her so happy she was almost sad. But lately, she had really begun to wonder about her name. Why was she named Sophie? She didn't know any other girls who were named Sophie. She wasn't sure if she liked her name. Someone could make it sound really weird—like Soapy, which led to Dopey, which would be really embarrassing. She finally decided to ask her mom if there was a really good reason why she had decided on Sophie.

Sophie knew she needed to ask this question at the right moment. She didn't want to ask her when she had a lot of time—like the time she asked about who God was. It was a really long story, and she was almost sorry she had asked, though her mom did help her understand a little bit about the subject. So…she thought maybe the best time to ask was in the morning before her mom went to work. Her mom was always in a hurry to get to work on time, but Sophie knew she would stop and talk to her for a little bit about something so important. The next morning, she ran upstairs to find out.

"Mom?"

"Good morning, dear Sophie."

(*She <u>always</u> says that!*)

"Why did you name me Sophie?"

"Oh, hon, you know I'm in a hurry to get to work." She paused for a moment and then sat down on the big comfy chair by her bed—a chair big enough for her mom, Sophie, *and* her sister, Elizabeth.

"Come…let's talk for a little bit." Sophie walked over and sat down, and her mom continued. "Well…let me see…how shall I start? When your dad and I knew you were going to be born and found out you were a little girl, we began to think about what we would name you. Names are really important, you know. A long time ago, in Bible days, names were considered windows to our hearts to help us know what kind of people we would be. So we began to ask the Lord to give us just the right name for you—one that you could be really comfortable with and yet one that you would grow into and enjoy. Of course, there are so many, many names! So I bought a book of names and, beginning with the As, started reading and studying about different ones that I thought might…"

"Mom?" Sophie interrupted.

"Yes, dear?"

"I know you have to go to work, and since S is number nineteen in the alphabet, maybe you should skip over to it."

Her mom really laughed—which puzzled Sophie. After her mom wiped the tears from her eyes (Sophie couldn't believe she thought it was *that* funny.), she continued.

"Well, the desire of my heart was that you would grow up to be a very wise and loving woman—someone who would know and learn so many, many things, whether about the Bible or history, languages or math, or how to tell jokes or how to dance wonderfully well."

"Really?" Sophie interrupted. "You know I love to dance, and I'm pretty good at math!"

Sophie's mom put her arm around her, gave her a hug, and said, "Yes, and I get so excited when I see you learning these things, and my desire is that you will come to know how wisdom can be used in all that you learn! Because, you see, wisdom is not just learning things. Wisdom is being able to use what you learn to bring honor to God first—and then to greatly enjoy life because you know how to use this knowledge to be happy and content…and…to help others to be happy and content also. Do you understand what it means to be content?"

"I think so," said Sophie, "doesn't that mean being sort of like satisfied with where you live and what you have?"

"Yes, that is a good way of putting it. By the time I got to the *S* and saw *Sophia*, I had found *the* name! Your name, Sophie, comes from the Greek word *Sophia*, which means 'wisdom—knowing and understanding the true nature of things.'"

"Wow!" interrupted Sophie, "that sounds great! But I'm not sure I know what that means."

Her mom paused and smiled. "Well, as I was saying, it is an adult way of saying that you will be able to understand what is true about God, His ways, and His people. When you understand what is true, you can become a wise and loving woman who loves others as Jesus loves you. Wisdom, Sophie, is like a beautiful jewel—a jewel that has many sides to it, all of which sparkle and shine and add to the beauty of all God has given us."

"But Mom," Sophie interrupted, "don't you think I need to be older before I can learn those kinds of things?"

"Well, that's the wonder about getting wisdom," said Sophie's mom. "Wisdom can begin at an early age because of what the Bible tells us about it. There is a wonderful verse for all of us that explains where wisdom starts. Let's read it together."

Sophie reached over to the lamp table and picked up her mom's Bible. "Where is it found?" she asked.

"In Proverbs 9:10," her mom replied.

Sophie knew where that book was because it was right after the Book of Psalms, which was in the middle of the Bible—so Proverbs was easy to find. After finding Proverbs, she went to Chapter 9, verse 10, and began reading to her mom, "The fear of the Lord is the beginning of wisdom, and knowledge of the Holy One is understanding." Sophie thought for a moment and then said, "I know the 'Holy One' is God…but…am I really supposed to be afraid of Him?"

"I think if we could see God, we probably would be frightened because He *is* so *big* and *powerful!*" Her mom paused for a moment and then continued, "He *is* the *One* and *Almighty God!* But it certainly doesn't mean that we are to live in terror of Him, Sophie. There are so many verses in the Bible that tell us how much He loves us and that we are forever safe with Him when we belong to Him. This might help you understand what I mean—do you remember when you were seven or eight years old, and we repainted our living room walls?"

Sophie sighed and said, "Oh yes…we were painting the walls a soft yellow color, and I really wanted to help you, and I was learning how…"

Her mom interrupted, "And what happened?"

"Your phone rang, and as you went into the kitchen to answer it, you told me not to do any more until you got back. I waited…but you were gone for a while…so I thought I could paint just a little bit by myself. As I was trying to get the paint, I stumbled and kicked over the can of paint…and the whole gallon of yellow paint came pouring out on our light brown carpet!"

"And how did that make you feel?" Sophie's mom asked.

"Oh!—I was *soooo* scared! I just wanted to run into my bedroom and hide! I knew I was in big-time trouble…and then you walked into the room."

"And why were you so scared?"

"Because I knew you had told me to leave the paint alone—and I had disobeyed!"

"So which was the harder…facing up to me or getting in trouble?"

"I'm not sure." Sophie thought about it for a few moments and then said, "I guess it was harder to face you because I knew I had really messed up! I don't think I understood that back then...I was only seven. But now that I think about it, I do think that was why I was so afraid."

Her mom paused for a moment and then said, "Were you afraid that I wouldn't love you anymore?"

"Oh no, Mom—I knew you loved me! I didn't even think of that! You have always told me I would be your little girl forever! It's just that... well...you're an adult, and I'm a child—and I know that you know more than me, and I wasn't doing what you wanted me to do, so I was just frightened and...and...Mom, is that sort of what it means to *fear the Lord*?"

"Ah, Sophie...it's just a tiny little bit of what it means! No one can really explain all the majesty and power of God, but it *is* true that God's power and wisdom are so very far above our own—and because we know that, we look at *Him* with great reverence, fear, and awe. And we also know that He is *the One* whose ability to forgive, to send peace, and to give joy is so much greater than our human minds can imagine, and we can live in joy and wonder at who He is and what He can do! And the good news is that since the fear of the Lord is the beginning of wisdom, it really doesn't matter how old we are when we start! We can even be a child! Jesus said, 'Let the children come unto me, for of such is the kingdom of heaven.'"

Sophie sat really still...for at least 6 seconds...and then looked up and said to her mom, "How do we ever understand all of that?"

"That is why Jesus came," replied her mom. "Jesus is God's Son, and Jesus came to earth and lived as a human being so He could reveal His Father to all of us! When we believe in Jesus, whose name means Savior, He shows us the way to God, and His Spirit lives in our hearts and minds and helps us to understand."

"*Hmmm*...That's a lot to wonder about, but I can see why wisdom is so important! So that's why you named me Sophie?"

"That's why, and we were right because you are already growing and learning to be wise. This weekend, I will write out some things for you about your name so you can have them to look at every once in a while. Now scoot—I have to get to work."

Sophie walked slowly down the stairs, thinking, *I wonder if everyone's names mean something…*

What Do You Think?

1. Tell me the first thing that comes into your mind when I say the following words: God, Jesus, Holy Spirit.
2. Why do you think Sophie was asking about wisdom?
3. Who needs wisdom? Why?
4. Would you like to know what your name means?

Prayer

Review Memory Verse: "The fear of the Lord is the beginning of wisdom, and knowledge of the Holy One is understanding" (Proverbs 9:10, NIV).

SUPPLY LIST FOR ACTIVITY 1

YouTube Video: "CREATION CALLS by Brian Doerksen," over four thousand views, posted two years ago on the channel "RC Schult."

* * *

Activity 1

Proverbs 9:10 is the theme of *Life with Sophie*. It is also the memory verse for this chapter. The intent of this activity is to help children see the wonder of the power, majesty, and great goodness of God. To see God in all of His power would be terribly frightening simply by the sheer magnitude of it. As great as His power is—as seen in the might of tornadoes, hurricanes, tsunamis, etc.—His power is also seen in the magnificence of nature's beauty and creative vastness. Therefore, while we want our children to see and, yes, even fear and have respect for the Lord, we also want them to see that His love, beauty, and never-failing faithfulness, which is so evident in the creation, are given in the same measure.

There are magnificent photographs and videos of nature and art available on a number of websites; YouTube has many! However, in my opinion, there is one that far exceeds all the others. It is an eight-minute video on YouTube by RC Schult entitled "CREATION CALLS by Brian Doerksen" Clips from the BBC movie *Earth* are used to express the creativity, beauty, and magnificence of God's creation, within which we are so blessed to live. It is a video that each member of the family will thoroughly enjoy! Even the two-year-old in our home was fascinated by it!

After viewing the video, spend some time talking with your children about what they have just seen. Ask simple questions like:

- What did you like best in the video? (Listen to their thoughts and insights, and then share yours.)
- What would you like to go and see if you could?

- Would you like to be a photographer and be able to take these pictures?
- What do these pictures tell us about God?

God is creative and artistic, has a great imagination, loves colors (He could have made everything black and white), is powerful, and loves us enough to make this beautiful world for us.

Following this discussion time, spend some time going over the memory verse and encourage them to memorize it. Review the memory verse several times before beginning the next chapter to be sure they have mastered it. Each chapter will present another memory verse.

Finally, pray with your family, asking the Lord to plant within each of them a great desire for wisdom.

Parent's Guide for Chapter 1
Devotional 1:
The Wisdom of Solomon

Emphasis

This devotional takes a look at the author of most of the Book of Proverbs. It highlights the amazing choice Solomon made when given the opportunity; but it also shows that even though Solomon's wisdom was tremendous and has been a great benefit to the church, he failed in the latter years of his life because he thought he could worship other gods while at the same time worshiping the One True God. Solomon's life is an excellent example of the failure we will always experience when we do not depend on the truth God reveals to us in Jesus.

Scripture Reading: "Do not forsake wisdom, and she will protect you; love her and she will watch over you" (Proverbs 4:6, NIV).

Suggested Answers to "What Do You Think?" Questions

1. King Solomon could have had anything he wanted, but he asked for wisdom. Why do you think he did that?

    The Bible does not give us that answer, but he must have loved and trusted God a lot and wanted only what was best for His people.

2. What happened as a result of his request?

    God gave Solomon wisdom so he could be a good king over God's people. Solomon did not ask for things for himself—and because of that, God also gave him riches and fame like the world had never seen before Solomon—or has ever seen since.

3. Why do you think Solomon drifted away from God?

   King Solomon was affected by money, possessions, and power. He began to think more about all the money and things that he had than he thought about God. He also had another huge problem: Solomon loved many, many women and married them all! These women were from countries that followed other gods, and his many wives persuaded him to worship their gods instead of the One True God—so Solomon forgot God's ways.

4. What can you learn from this?

   When you take your eyes off Jesus, it gradually becomes easier and easier to forget about "truth" and the way God wants you to live!

Chapter 1 Devotional 1: The Wisdom of Solomon

Scripture Reading: "Do not forsake wisdom and she will protect you; love her, and she will watch over you" (Proverbs 4:6, NIV).

"You know what, Mom?" said Sophie.

Sophie's mom smiled and replied, "What, Sophie?"

"King Solomon wrote Proverbs!"

"And just how did you learn that?" said her mom.

"Mrs. Hanson told us yesterday in Sunday school. She was telling us how the Bible was written—and that there were forty authors for all sixty-six books! So, since the memory verse that I'm learning is in Proverbs, I asked her who wrote Proverbs, and she said it was written by King Solomon. I found Proverbs in my Bible, and there—right in the middle of the first verse of Chapter One—it tells you that Solomon was the son of David, King of Israel. Then I told her that we were learning about Proverbs at home, and she said she thought that was a great idea because it is a book about wisdom."

"Did she tell you how King Solomon knew all about wisdom?" asked her mom.

"No…why? Do you know how?"

"Well…Yes, I do! It had to do with an amazing dream in which God visited Solomon and asked him what he would like to receive from God."

"You mean God actually came to King Solomon in a dream?" said Sophie.

"Yes," replied her mom. "He did come to Solomon in a dream! However, the story also says that Solomon loved the Lord, so the Lord knew that Solomon's request would be an unselfish one."

"*Wow!*" exclaimed Sophie. "What did King Solomon want?"

"The answer just might surprise you! He could have been tempted to ask for riches, or lands, or honor—yet he did not. Instead, because he loved the Lord, King Solomon asked for an understanding heart so he would be able to judge the people well and know the difference between good and evil."

"Really? He could have asked for anything…and *that* was what he wanted?" asked Sophie. "He must have been a good man, so God gave him a wise heart."

"Indeed—He did! As you can imagine, it pleased the Lord very much. He gave Solomon a very wise heart—a heart that was like no other heart before him. And because he didn't ask for riches or honor, God gave those things to him too!"

Sophie was quiet for a moment and then said, "Do you think I could ask God for a wise heart?"

"I think that would please Him very much. God tells us in Proverbs that if we look for wisdom as though it were silver and search for it as we would for hidden treasure, then we will understand what is good and right because wisdom will enter our hearts."

"And that is what King Solomon did, didn't he, Mom? Was he always wise?"

Sophie's mom sighed and said, "No, I'm sorry to say that King Solomon wasn't always wise. In fact, in his later years, he did not act wisely at all. Solomon had many wives and…"

"*Many wives!*" interrupted Sophie. "I thought the Bible said a man should only have one wife!"

"Well, that was after Jesus came, but it still became a huge problem for King Solomon. Most of his wives were from foreign countries…with foreign gods…"

"*Foreign gods!*" interrupted Sophie again. "That doesn't sound wise at all!"

"You're right again," replied her mom, "it wasn't wise at all! That is why when the Lord blesses us with His knowledge and understanding; it is so important to realize that it isn't just the knowledge and understanding that makes us wise; it is the power of His Holy Spirit living within us that gives us the strength to *do* what He teaches us."

Sophie was quiet for a little bit and then said, "They didn't have Jesus then, did they, Mom?"

"No," replied her mom, "not in the way we have Him. Jesus has always been the Son of God, but He had not yet come into the world as a human being to die for our sins and be resurrected. We know that after Jesus was resurrected and went back to heaven, He sent the Holy Spirit to live within us and to guide us. The people in the Old Testament didn't have the Holy Spirit to guide them like we do!"

"I feel sorry for King Solomon!"

"Yes, I know, but God did give him great wisdom and understanding…and we all still benefit from that today. Perhaps God wants us to realize an even bigger lesson—that even when we have knowledge and understanding, the *wisdom* that comes from that is only found when we follow Jesus…who truly *is* the author of wisdom!"

"Well then, when I ask for a wise heart, I will ask for that too!" Sophie said.

"Why don't we ask together—for regardless of our age, we all need the wisdom that comes from following Jesus?"

What Do You Think?

1. King Solomon could have had anything he wanted, but he asked for wisdom. Why do you think he did that?
2. What happened as a result of his request?
3. Why do you think Solomon drifted away from God?
4. What can you learn from this?

Prayer

Review Memory Verse: "The fear of the Lord is the beginning of wisdom, and knowledge of the Holy One is understanding" (Proverbs 9:10, NIV).

Parent's Guide for Chapter 1 Devotional 2: What Is Fear of the Lord?

Emphasis

This devotional explains what is meant by "reverent fear." The *Maid of the Mist* excursion boat at Niagara Falls is used as an example of tremendous power that will produce reverent fear. The short video of Niagara Falls can be found at www.maidofthemist.com, and if possible, you should show this to your children. It gives a great explanation of the power of the Falls and is an exciting and beautiful video to see. It can be shown before or after reading the devotional. When you are reading about the power of the boat against the Falls with younger children, you might want to slow down and use hand motions to explain what is happening.

Scripture Reading: "By wisdom the Lord laid the earth's foundations, by understanding He set the heavens in place; by His knowledge the watery depths were divided, and the clouds let drop the dew" (Proverbs 3:19–20, NIV).

Suggested Answers to "What Do You Think?" Questions

1. Have you ever been on the *Maid of the Mist*? Would you like to go?

    Parents, if your children have taken this trip, ask them what the most exciting thing was that they can remember. If they have not been on this trip, ask them what they think the most exciting thing would be.

2. What does "reverent fear" mean?

   Having a real sense of fear or being in awe at something or someone who is much more powerful than you—like standing on a small boat that is heading toward a huge waterfall, like we just saw in the Niagara Falls video. However, this kind of fear is not a fear that makes us feel "terror"; we simply feel amazed and in awe at how big and powerful God is—and how small we are! Just like we can trust the captain of the boat to keep us safe, we can also put our trust in Jesus, the greatest captain who ever lived! When Jesus comes into your life to stay, He becomes the captain of your life—and He promises to guide you and bring you safely through all the problems in your life.

Chapter 1 Devotional 2: What Is Fear of the Lord?

Scripture Reading: "By wisdom the Lord laid the earth's foundations, by understanding He set the heavens in place; by His knowledge the watery depths were divided, and the clouds let drop the dew" (Proverbs 3:19–20, NIV).

"Sophie," her mom said, "Do you know what a reverent fear is?"

Sophie had been reading her library book and looked up at her mom. "Did you say rever…rever…some kind of fear?"

"A reverent fear," replied her mom.

"Well," Sophie thought for a minute, "I'm not sure…but I've learned the memory verse; you want to hear it?"

"Certainly," said her mother.

Sophie took a deep breath and said, "The fear of the Lord is the beginning of wisdom, and knowledge of the Holy One is understanding" (Proverbs 9:10, NIV).

"That's wonderful!—and remember, we talked about what it means to fear the Lord, didn't we?"

"Yes," Sophie replied…but…how do we have a *reverent* fear?

Elizabeth, who had been doing her homework, now joined the conversation. "A reverent fear is somewhat confusing, Mom. We know what reverence means, and we know what fear means—but putting them together does seem a little odd."

"Yeah, like Jackson saying, 'Look at my *great* worms,' yuck!" interrupted Sophie.

Their mom laughed at Sophie. "Well, perhaps I can explain a little better. You're right, Elizabeth; the two words don't seem to go together at first glance. Reverence means to highly honor and respect someone or something—a kind of *wow* or amazement deep inside us—while fear is a feeling that something bad is going to happen to us or to someone we love. When the expression 'fear the Lord' is used in the Bible, there certainly is an awareness of fear in His power and might and…"

"Yes," interrupted Sophie. "We talked about that too, didn't we? It reminded me of when I spilled the paint, and I was so afraid!"

"Yes, something like that. I've been looking at the website of *the Maid of the Mist* at Niagara Falls, and I thought it gave a great example of reverent fear."

Sophie and Elizabeth got up and went over to where their mom was looking at the computer. "Can we see too?" they both asked.

"Sure," their mom continued. "Look at this advertisement video. When you are on that boat gazing at this mighty waterfall, it is then that I believe you experience a reverent fear—because you not only *see* the majesty of the waterfall, you can *hear* the power of it, too! Now you *know* that the Falls would be very dangerous if you were to get too close—but you also *know* that you are in *the Maid of the Mist*, where you are safe because the captain has already explained why there is no danger! Now look…see how close the boat is to the Falls? With all the power that its engine can produce, the boat goes as close as it can until the much greater power of the water coming over the Falls becomes more powerful than the manmade power of the engine. When that happens, the boat cannot go any farther, and it turns around and heads back to where it started."

The girls were watching the video and listening intently, so their mom continued. "Let's pretend for a moment that the *Maid of the Mist* represents the 'Ship of Life' on which each one of us travels. We can also pretend that the mighty waterfall represents the power and majesty of God. We might be tempted to boldly say, 'I know I can steer my ship in the right direction all by myself…and I'm just going to keep working and working at it!' What do you think would happen?"

Sophie looked at her mom and said, "Oh...that would be awful! What a mess I would make!"

Then Elizabeth spoke up and said, "I would be terrified!"

"I feel the same way, girls! But when we ask Jesus to come into our lives, we are also asking Him to be the captain of our lives. Then we never need to be terrified because we can trust Him to guide our lives through every storm or problem that we face.

You know...if people could somehow see the mighty power and strength of God, I think there *would* be a sense of fear. However, when Jesus is in control of our lives, that 'fear' is not a *terror*; that 'fear' is simply an overwhelming feeling of awe and amazement at how powerful God really is! To me...that is *reverent fear*! From everything people have told me about Niagara Falls, it has to be truly awesome to see—to the point where you just want to be silent and take it all in. Do you understand a little better what it means to have a *reverent fear*?"

And together, both girls exclaimed, "We sure do! When can we go?"

What Do You Think?

1. Have you ever been on the *Maid of the Mist*? Would you like to go?
2. What does "reverent fear" mean?

Prayer

Review Memory Verse: "The fear of the Lord is the beginning of wisdom, and knowledge of the Holy One is understanding" (Proverbs 9:10, NIV).

Parent's Guide for Chapter 1 Devotional 3: What Comes after *the Beginning*?

Emphasis

If the "fear of the Lord" is the beginning, what comes next? The emphasis is to help children see that God is an encompassing presence that deeply loves and cares for us individually. As we increasingly know more about Him (the "knowledge of the Holy One"), our understanding will continue to grow, our lives will be richer, and our ability to help others will be greatly multiplied.

Scripture Reading: "Who has gone up to heaven and come down? Whose hands have gathered up the wind? Who has wrapped up the waters in his cloak? Who has established all the ends of the earth? What is His name, and what is the name of His son? Surely you know! Every word of God is flawless; He is a shield to those who take refuge in Him" (Proverbs 30:4–5, NIV).

Suggested Answers to "What Do You Think?" Questions

1. What did Sophie discover about knowledge and understanding?

    "Knowledge" is what you know about something or someone. "Understanding" is what you get <u>after</u> you know the facts about something or <u>after</u> you have known someone for a long time.

2. Fill in the blanks: The more you <u>know</u> about the Lord, the more you will understand just how much He <u>*loves you!*</u>

3. Who is the writer talking about in your scripture reading today? What is His name and the name of His Son?

   God—Jesus is the name of God's Son!

4. He promises to be a shield and a refuge for all those who come to Him. In battle, what did the shield provide? What does "refuge" mean?

   The shield provided "protection." A "refuge" is a strong place of shelter where nothing can harm you.

Chapter 1 Devotional 3: What Comes after *the Beginning?*

Sophie had just put her pajamas on and crawled into bed. While she waited for her mom to pray with her before going to sleep, she was saying her memory verse to herself, "The fear of the Lord is the beginning of wisdom, hmmm…the beginning…I wonder…" Her mom interrupted her thoughts as she came into the room.

"Mom?" Sophie said.

"Yes?" her mom replied.

"What comes after the beginning?" Sophie questioned.

"The beginning of what?" her mom said.

"You know…the beginning of wisdom? If the fear of the Lord is the beginning of wisdom, what comes next?"

Sophie's mom smiled and said, "That's a great question, but the answer is in the next part, though you do have to kind of think about it."

"Oh," said Sophie, "you mean the part about the knowledge of the Lord being understanding?"

"Exactly," her mom replied. "What is knowledge?"

"*Mommmm*, I know what knowledge is—it's what you know about something or someone…Oh [she paused and thought a moment], so I guess the more we know about the Lord, the more we understand what wisdom is—right?"

"That's right," said Sophie's mom, "and the more we know about the Lord, the more we understand how deeply He loves us and wants us to learn about His ways because those are the ways that will make our lives so much better. And not just our lives! As we know more about His wisdom, we will be able to help others also."

Sophie thought for a minute and then said, "Okay, I think I'll wonder about all of that after you pray."

Sophie's mom smiled and said, "Good, I think that's a great idea!" Then she prayed for Sophie that she would be able to learn more and more about God's wisdom as she learned more and more about His great love for her.

Scripture Reading: "Who has gone up to heaven and come down? Whose hands have gathered up the wind? Who has wrapped up the waters in a cloak? Who has established all the ends of the earth? What is His name, and what is the name of His son? Surely you know! Every word of God is flawless; He is a shield to those who take refuge in Him" (Proverbs 30:4–5, NIV).

What Do You Think?

1. What did Sophie discover about knowledge and understanding?
2. Fill in the blanks: The more you _____ about the Lord, the more you will _____ how much He _____.
3. Who is the writer talking about in your scripture reading today? What is His name and the name of His Son?
4. He promises to be a shield and a refuge for all those who come to Him. In battle, what did the shield provide? What does "refuge" mean?

"The fear of the Lord is the beginning of wisdom, and knowledge of the Holy One is understanding" (Proverbs 9:10, NIV).

CHAPTER 2:
Treasuring a Good Name

Parent's Guide for Chapter 2: Treasuring a Good Name

Emphasis

Chapter 2 introduces Elizabeth Grace, Sophie's fifteen-year-old sister. Sophie learns the meaning of Elizabeth's name, and her mom explains each of their names during a family time, where they make posters about their names. The chapter emphasizes the value of a good name and the value God places upon each individual child.

Memory Verse: "A good name is more desirable than great riches; to be esteemed is better than silver or gold" (Proverbs 22:1, NIV).

Also introduced in Chapter 2 is the sorrow Sophie carries because of her parents' divorce.

Suggested Answers to "What Do You Think?" Questions

1. Why is a good name more desirable than great riches?

    When people think about you or hear your name, you want them to have good thoughts about you. Money cannot make that happen! You can have so much money that you can buy anything you want, but if you treat people badly or tell lies about them, they still won't like you. On the other hand, you might be poor with very little money, but if you are nice to people and love them the way God loves, you will have many friends because people will want to spend time with you. The kind of person you are is more important than how much money you have.

2. What does it mean to be "esteemed"?

    It means people like you, think good thoughts about you, appreciate you, and have good feelings when they think about you. Would you like people to feel this way about you?

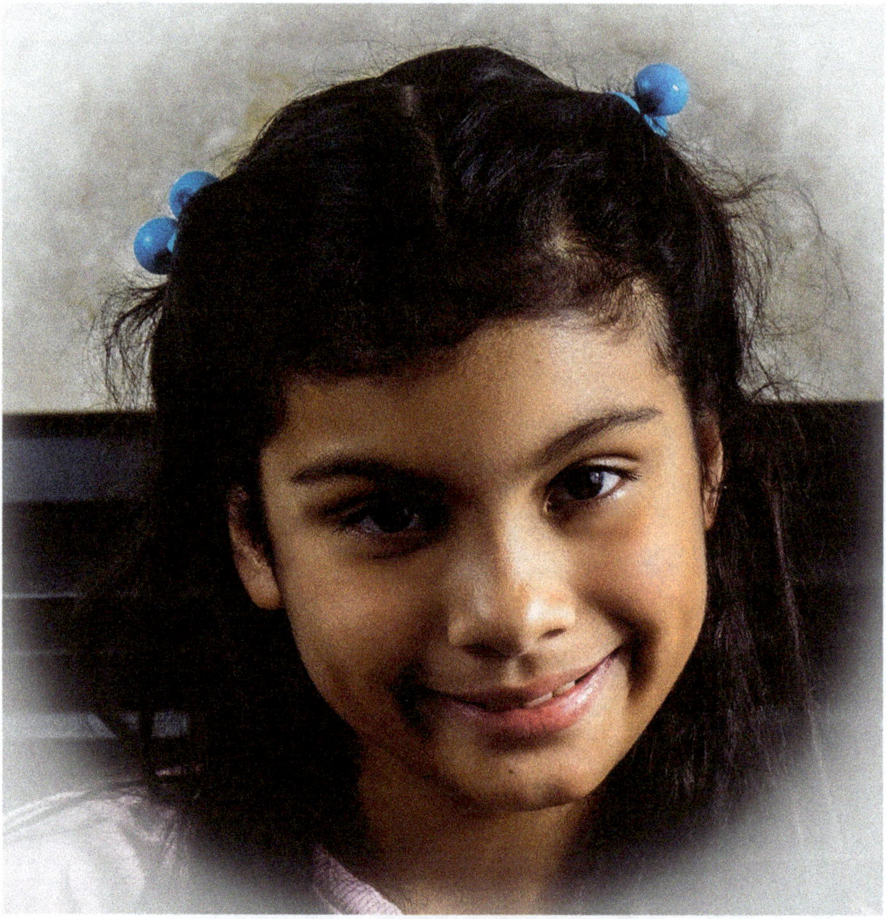

Chapter Two:
Treasuring a Good Name

My sister, Elizabeth Grace, is my best friend! She is fifteen years old, however, and she can be *sooooo* bossy at times! She is really, really pretty and has a lot of friends—*and* she has a boyfriend! Well, I guess he's a boyfriend—they aren't allowed to go anywhere by themselves. But they can hang out with other friends, and he comes over sometimes, and they watch a movie and eat popcorn…and that is when she gets so bossy. It's like, all of a sudden, I don't live here anymore! "Sophie, you can't come in here. This movie is way too adult for you." "Sophie, this popcorn is not for you." "Sophie, I think it's your bedtime." Boy, you would think I was four years old!

Most of the time, though, Elizabeth's really cool! She even helps me sometimes with my homework. She takes me to the mall, and we look in all the stores, especially the ones that smell good—like *The Bath Shop*. We go in and try all the body lotion samples, like *Fresh Mint* and *Lavender*—and I love the *Grapefruit*! Sometimes we go to the movies together, and sometimes we ride our bikes together. But my favorite times are when she lets me come into her bedroom, and she does my fingernails, and we just "talk" about sister stuff. Those are the best times, and I think I will always remember them even when I am *really old*—like maybe twenty-five.

After Mom told me what my name meant, I wondered about Elizabeth's name. So when we left for school, I asked her if she knew the meaning of *her* name.

"Yes, Sophie Anne [my mom always calls me 'dear Sophie' and my sister always calls me 'Sophie Anne'], Mom told me several years ago; I think about it every once in a while. I like what my name means, and some great women have had my name and have done some wonderful things, starting with Elizabeth in the Bible, who was John the Baptist's mother."

"Did Mom tell you what your name meant when you were my age?" I asked.

"Yes, I guess she did. I remember asking her and Dad about it. You must have been four or five then."

"So that was before Mom and Dad separated, wasn't it?" I asked.

"Yes, it was…you really miss Dad, don't you?" asked Elizabeth.

"Uh-huh," I said. "I guess I'm getting used to it more now—it's been almost two years…but I wish he lived closer so we could see him more often. It's hard for me to remember the times we were all together, but it helps when you, Mom, and I do things together."

"Well," said Elizabeth, "this morning, Mom told me you had asked about your name, and she told me that we are going to do something tonight to help us understand our names better. She told me a little about it, and it should be fun. I'll help you with yours if you want me to."

"Oh, that would be great, Elizabeth—thank you!" I exclaimed.

"And I miss Dad too, Sophie; some things are just hard to understand, aren't they?"

"Yes," I said. "It still hurts and makes me sad, but it does really help when we have family times. I wonder what Mom is planning this time?"

"I'm not sure," said Elizabeth, "but we'll make it a fun time—and knowing Mom, she probably has it all planned out," said Elizabeth.

When Mom came in from work, her arms were full of packages. There was colored paper—really colored, like lime green, sunshine yellow, hot pink, grass green, purple, and sky blue. She also had sparkly stickers shaped like stars, butterflies, and flowers—and colored pens, glue, tape, and two picture frames.

After dinner, we put all of the things Mom bought out on the table, and then Mom said, "I took some time today to gather information on the meaning of your names and to think about Bible verses that would remind you of your names. I also found some of God's promises to help you remember those meanings. I thought that a good project for each of you would be to make a small poster with your name and its meaning on it, along with the Bible verses. Then you can each decorate your poster with bright colors, put it in the picture frame, and hang it in your room or put it on your dresser. What do you think?"

Elizabeth wasn't quite as excited as I was because she already knew what her name meant, but she said she was okay with it. Mom pulled out two sheets of paper containing our names. "I'll start with you, Elizabeth," and she began to read: "The name *Elizabeth* refers to God's great abundance, and the name *Grace* refers to the inner beauty of one who gives mercy and favor. When we put the two names together, along with the ideas we see in Psalm 118:29 about the goodness of God and Hebrews 4:16 about the grace that God continues to give us, we have your wonderful name, *Elizabeth Grace*, which means:

'One who trusts in the abundance of God and rejoices in giving mercy and loving-kindness.'"

Then she turned to me and said, "Okay, Sophie, now let's look at yours."

She picked up the other sheet of paper, and Elizabeth and I looked on as she read: "*Sophie*, from the Greek word *Sophia*, is all about one who seeks wisdom, while *Anne* comes from the Hebrew origin meaning 'grace of God.' The verses I chose for you that speak of these two meanings are found in Proverbs 3:4, which speaks of seeking wisdom, and 2 Corinthians 12:9, which refers to the rich supply of grace that God continues to give us even in our many weaknesses. When we put your beautiful names together, we come up with this meaning for *Sophie Anne*:

'One who seeks wisdom with kindness, grace, and beauty.' So, girls, here are all the supplies. Why don't you get started and see what you can do with all of this *stuff* I brought home?"

Mom began to get busy in the kitchen, but I knew she would be too curious to leave us alone completely. After a little while, she would come back and check on us—but she was always encouraging, so it was okay. It took some time to get the posters just the way we wanted; but when we were all done, we put them in the picture frames, and they looked like this:

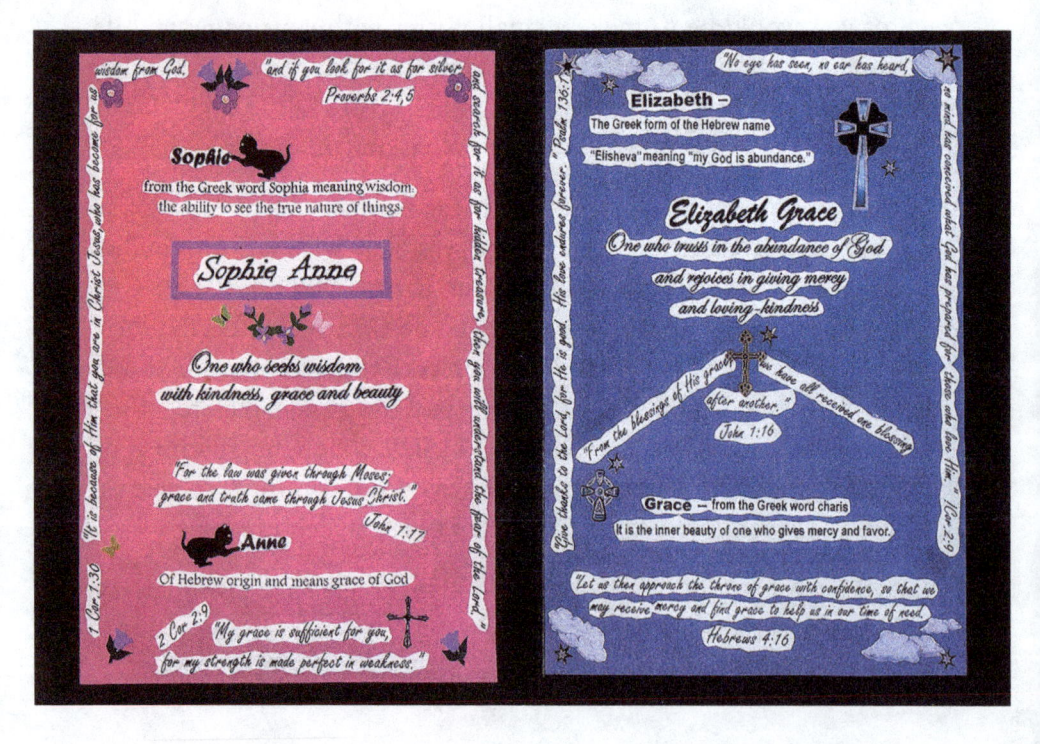

We called Mom to come and see, so she came in and *oohed* and *aahed* over them (you know how moms are)—but we were kind of proud of them too! Then she held the pictures up and said, "You both did so well!" She turned to Elizabeth and said, "Elizabeth, we have talked about your name before, but this is a good time to remind you of how uniquely wonderful you are to all of us—and especially to God! The older you become, the more I see how your name fits you, for I see a young woman who is increasingly learning that God is someone you can trust and who is with you day by day. Just last week, when we were discussing how expensive college tuition is…what was it, you said?"

Elizabeth smiled and said, "Well, that I had begun to put a part of my babysitting money aside, and that I would continue to do that when I was old enough to work—and that I sort of thought God would take care of us when that time came."

Mom reached over and gave Elizabeth a hug. "Absolutely, and while I see you understanding more of His goodness, I also see the grace and beauty that comes with that kind of wisdom."

Then Mom turned to me and said, "Sophie Anne, your name is also one that fits you so well. You are inquisitive, vivacious, and always wondering about life and why things are the way they are. It is this very quality that is one of the starting points of wisdom. I remember that even as a little girl of five or six, you wanted to know what was before God. That was several years ago, but do you remember that?"

"Oh yes, I do," I said, "because sometimes at night, especially when I look out my window and see the moon and stars, I still wonder about it. You told me that it was a great mystery but that there wasn't a time 'before God' because God has always been and always will be. It's kind of a funny answer, but it still makes me feel good. Maybe that's one way you can tell if an answer is true because it seems to fit the question…you think so, Mom?"

Mom gave me a hug then and said, "Yes, I think that's one way of looking at it, but I also think that it might have something to do with grace and truth being found in Jesus. He gives His grace, and then we can understand more about His truth."

"I don't think I know what that means, but I am really getting sleepy," I said.

Mom could see that we were both tired—and so was she. So she prayed for us and told us it was time to go to bed.

Elizabeth and I took our pictures to our rooms; Elizabeth hung hers on the wall with some of her favorite pictures, but I put mine on the lamp table by my bed. I put my pajamas on, brushed my teeth, and got into bed. Then I lay there thinking about what we did. The last thing I remember before I went to sleep was saying, "Lord, my mom is kind of neat… *Thank You*—and will You help me become what my name means?"

What Do You Think?

1. Why is a good name more desirable than great riches?
2. What does it mean to be "esteemed"?

Prayer

Memory Verse: "A good name is more desirable than great riches; to be esteemed is better than silver or gold" (Proverbs 22:1, NIV).

SUPPLY LIST FOR ACTIVITY 2

- Colorful computer or construction paper
- Stickers (stars, butterflies, flowers, etc.)
- Colorful pens, felt-tip markers, glue, tape
- A frame
- Book: *The Name Book* by Dorothy Astoria (found new or used on Amazon.com) or
- Website to Use: meaningofnames.com

* * *

Activity 2

This is one of two activities that may require an hour or so of preparation. Though it takes a little longer than the other activities, it is one that will help children recognize how truly unique they are and will also solidify the connection with you as the parent.

All children want to know that they are part of *the plan* and that they are not only very special but known by God even before they are born. In Isaiah 43:1 (NIV), we read, "I have redeemed you; I have called you by name; you are mine." Even if parents do not pick their child's name with an understanding of what it means or the impact a name can have on their child, God knew while the child was still in the mother's womb what that child's name would be. It does not matter if the child is adopted—God is still sovereign! This activity involves researching each child's name to discover what it means and providing biblical applications that will help each child understand the significance of his or her name.

There is an excellent book (listed above) that gives the meaning, origins, and spiritual significance of thousands of names, along with excellent scripture verses. A website giving the origin and meaning of names is also listed above.

If you, as a parent, feel that another scripture more aptly fits your child, that verse is the one you should use.

Once you have this information and the supplies, which are also listed above, plan for an evening of fun as they put their names and verses together in picture form for their own rooms. This is an inexpensive project; you only need two or three packages of stickers or decorative appliqués, felt-tip markers, and brightly colored computer paper. Frames that are 8" x 10" seem to work best and are large enough to contain all the information yet not too large to put on a chest or dresser or to hang on a wall. You will need to help younger children by steering them into a cohesive pattern so the meanings go with the verses, etc.

When you have the names and their meanings written out, spend some time alone with each child going over the meanings (perhaps after they go to bed). Explain not only what his or her name means but the verses you have chosen to go along with the names. This would be a great time to pray with each child, giving thanks that God chose to put him or her in your family.

As a side note, if in your family you have older children who feel this activity is too juvenile for them, you could encourage them to make something very understated—perhaps calligraphy on a good vellum 5" x 7" card that could be framed. This would be a reminder to them of the value you put on their names and the appreciation you have for their uniqueness.

Prayer

Memory Verse: "A good name is more desirable than great riches; to be esteemed is better than silver or gold" (Proverbs 22:1, NIV).

Parent's Guide for Chapter 2 Devotional 1: What Does God's Name Mean?

Emphasis

This devotional has a twofold purpose: (1) to help children see that God has many names, all having to do with the multitude of attributes of His Person, which help us understand the different ways He comes to us in our need; and (2) to help children see the need to be understanding of the faults of others, to forgive others, and to be quick to ask others to forgive them.

Scripture Reading: "The name of the Lord is a fortified tower; the righteous run to it and are safe" (Proverbs 18:10, NIV).

Suggested Answers to "What Do You Think?" Questions

1. Your scripture reading says, "The name of the Lord is a strong tower; the righteous run to it and are safe." What does "a strong tower" mean?

   A strong tower means a sturdy, well-built shelter that protects you and won't fall down—like a storm shelter, where you can be safe in a hurricane.

2. Sophie remembers getting angry with her friend and not sharing her Barbies with her. She said she needed to ask Jesus to forgive her when she is selfish with her friends. When she asks

Jesus to forgive her, how does she know He does?

She can know because she went to the Lord (her strong tower that protects her and keeps her safe) and told Him what she had done and asked Him to forgive her. Jesus said He will always forgive and keep you safe.

Memory Verse: "A good name is more desirable than great riches; to be esteemed is better than silver or gold" (Proverbs 22:1, NIV).

Chapter 2 Devotional 1: What Does God's Name Mean?

Scripture Reading: "The name of the Lord is a fortified tower; the righteous run to it and are safe" (Proverbs 18:10, NIV).

Sophie's mom was making lunches while Sophie was eating breakfast. They had been talking about the name posters the girls had made the night before. Sophie's mom told her again how well she thought they both had done.

Sophie nodded and said, "Thank you, it was fun to do, and I saw my picture as soon as I woke up this morning. But you know what? It makes me wonder about God's name. What does His name mean? We found out what our names mean, and you said He knew what our names would be before we were born—but we didn't talk about what His name means."

"That's a good question, but did you know that God has many names? Remember that God is One God—but He is Three in One! He's God the *Father*, as Jesus referred to Him many times; He's God the *Son*, Jesus the Christ, whose name means Savior; and He is God the *Holy Spirit*, often referred to as the Comforter. God is mostly referred to by Jewish people as Yahweh: a name used nearly 7,000 times in the Bible."

"That's a lot!" exclaimed Sophie, "but what does that mean?"

"Well, there are some questions as to the first time it was used, but the one where it was described so powerfully was when God came to Moses in the *burning bush* story..."

"Oh—I remember that," interrupted Sophie. "God told him to take off his shoes 'cause he was on holy ground."

"Yes, and Moses wanted to know what he should call Him when the Israelites asked who spoke to him. God told Moses to tell them He was I AM THAT I AM and that 'I AM has sent me to you.'"

"*Mooooom*, what does *that* mean?" asked Sophie.

"Well, in very simple terms, I think it means that God (I AM THAT I AM) is the absolute and unchanging Creator of all that is or will ever be in this universe. Plus, He has many traits that show His love and interest in all He has created. In other words, He is a very personal God who cares deeply for all people."

"*Soooo*, did the people understand that back then? And did He have more names? And wouldn't that be confusing?" asked Sophie.

"I can see why you would think that," said her mom, "but remember that we have the Holy Spirit who lives in our hearts to help us know His ways—in the Old Testament, it was different. People depended more on their leaders, to whom God spoke in order to lead their way. But God's ear has always heard the prayers of people who cried out to Him. And when He did, He was often referred to in the manner in which He helped them."

"Like who?" questioned Sophie.

"Well, I always think of Hagar when I think of someone who was terribly frightened and called upon God. Do you remember her?"

"I think I remember hearing her name, but I don't remember the story," said Sophie.

"But you remember Abraham and Sarah, don't you?"

"Oh sure—she was the one who was so old when she had a baby, wasn't she? That was pretty weird, but they were really happy about it, weren't they?"

Smiling, Sophie's mom replied, "Yes, they were *really* happy about it! It fulfilled a promise made to them years before that this baby, Isaac, would be the one from whom the Messiah would come. But when it didn't happen even after many years, Sarah told Abraham to take a second wife, her servant Hagar, who could perhaps have a son."

Shirley Porter

"Mom!" cried Sophie. "That's against the law—plus it's ridiculous! Why did she think she could do something about it?"

"She was just like all of us; sometimes we think we have to help God out. It wasn't against the law in those days, but it was a big mistake! After Hagar had a son, Sarah became jealous, and eventually, Hagar and her son were sent away. They wandered in the desert and were dying from thirst—and Hagar cried out to God. God heard her cry and came to them and opened her eyes so she could see that He was with her; then, He provided a well of water. So Hagar said, 'You are *El Roi*,' which means *the God who sees me*. Hagar made a home in that place and raised her son, Ishmael."

Sophie thought for a moment and then said, "Mom, that makes me angry with Sarah and Abraham. That was not right!"

Sophie's mom had been making their lunch when she paused and then sat down with Sophie at the table, took her face in her hands for a moment, looked into her eyes, and said, "Oh my dear Sophie, it will help you so much if you learn early in life that we all make mistakes! We all sin, and sometimes we pay dearly for those sins—but the wonderful news is that God knows us deeply and is always interested in showing us that He loves us and wants to provide a way for us. Yes, Abraham and Sarah were foolish and, in our way of thinking, deeply unkind to Hagar, but God is not threatened or worried, nor does He shake His head and say, 'Now what am I going to do?' He has a plan for each of us, and even when we sin and make mistakes, He is so very faithful to provide a new way that will still accomplish His plan for our good and for His glory. Does that help a little?"

Sophie thought for a moment and then hugged her mom and said, "Yes, it makes me remember that I got angry with Mary Sue last week and wouldn't let her play with my Barbies—and it made her very sad. And then I told her I was sorry and we had a good time together. I guess I need to remember to ask Jesus to forgive me when I do something like that, don't I?"

"Yes, that is always very wise. And He always hears and is ready to forgive. Remember…His name is *Jesus*, and *He* will save *His* people from their sins."

What Do You Think?

1. Your scripture reading says, "The name of the Lord is a fortified tower; the righteous run to it and are safe." What does "a fortified tower" mean?
2. Sophie remembers getting angry with her friend and not sharing her Barbies with her. She wanted to ask Jesus to forgive her when she is selfish with her friends. When she asks Jesus to forgive her, how does she know He does?

Prayer

Memory Verse: "A good name is more desirable than great riches; to be esteemed is better than silver or gold" (Proverbs 22:1, NIV).

Parent's Guide for Chapter 2
Devotional 2:
What's in a Name?

Emphasis

To help our children see that our names represent who we are to people we know, which means that desiring a "good" name is a worthwhile goal.

Scripture Reading: "A good name is more desirable than great riches; to be esteemed is better than silver or gold" (Proverbs 22:1, NIV).

Suggested Answers to "What Do You Think?" Questions

1. The saleslady was really embarrassed by what had happened to her. Has someone ever embarrassed you? Have you ever seen someone else embarrassed or bullied? Would you want someone to remember you that way?

    You may have to help in this area. Embarrassment is usually accidental; bullying is on purpose!

2. Sophie's mom tells her that our names mean more than just our identity. What does that mean?

    Who you are!

3. Sophie says that a "good name" means more than just its definition. What does that mean?

   Go over the definition of each child's name. Saying the meaning (or definition) of our name is just saying "words"! To actually <u>have</u> a good name means that you behave according to what your name means—so that when people think about your name, they have good memories.

4. Suppose the saleslady's teacher's name was "Elaine," which means "admirable, honorable, and good." Is that the way the saleslady remembered her?

   No—just the opposite! Her name meant one thing, but she acted very differently from its definition. If she had acted admirably in her words and actions, the saleslady might have continued her lessons and remembered her teacher as a nice person who encouraged her.

Memory Verse: "A good name is more desirable than great riches; to be esteemed is better than silver or gold" (Proverbs 22:1, NIV).

Chapter 2 Devotional 2: What's in a Name?

It must have been a slow day in the store because the saleslady was very talkative as she put the dress and scarf that Sophie wanted in the bag. She smiled at Sophie. "You picked out some lovely things," she said. "Are you going to do something special?"

Sophie smiled back and said, "Yes, I'm going to a recital that one of my best friends is going to be in."

"Really?" replied the lady. "I was in a piano recital once, but I made some mistakes and decided I wouldn't ever be in another one and pleaded with my mom to let me stop lessons. She knew I was really embarrassed, and she probably shouldn't have, but she let me quit."

"That's sad," said Sophie, "everyone makes mistakes."

"You're right," replied the saleslady, "and it *was* foolish! I regretted it later, but my teacher was young and didn't handle it well. She really scolded me, and it felt like she kind of made fun of me. She moved away shortly after that, and I never saw her again. But I won't ever forget her name. Every time I hear that name, I'm reminded of that embarrassing afternoon."

Another customer came to the counter and needed attention, so Sophie's mom paid for the merchandise and then said, "Thank you—and you know, it's never too late to try again. My mother decided to take organ lessons when she was in her fifties, and she did really well. Maybe you could give it a try."

The saleslady laughed and said, "You could be right—maybe I will!"

Sophie and her mom left the store, and Sophie looked up at her mom and said, "Whoa! She talked a lot, didn't she? I hope her teacher's name wasn't Sophie, Elizabeth, or Cynthia. I sure wouldn't want anyone to hear our names and be reminded of bad memories."

"You're right; our names say a lot more than just our identities, don't they?"

"Yes, I guess they do. A good name does mean more than *just its definition!*"

What Do You Think?

1. The saleslady was really embarrassed by what had happened to her. Has someone ever embarrassed you? Have you ever seen someone else embarrassed or bullied? Would you want someone to remember you that way?
2. Sophie's mom tells her that our names mean more than just our identity. What does that mean? Sophie says that a "good name" means more than just its definition. What does that mean?
3. Suppose the saleslady's teacher's name was "Elaine," which means "admirable, honorable, and good." Is that the way the saleslady remembered her?

Prayer

Memory Verse: "A good name is more desirable than great riches; to be esteemed is better than silver or gold" (Proverbs 22:1, NIV).

Parent's Guide for Chapter 2 Devotional 3:
The Old Pictures

Emphasis

To reiterate that our names represent our character and can leave the "fragrance of Christ" or perhaps a not-so-fragrant memory!

Scripture Reading: "Let love and faithfulness never leave you; bind them around your neck, write them on the tablet of your heart. Then you will win favor and a good name in the sight of God and man" (Proverbs 3:3–4, NIV).

Suggested Answers to "What Do You Think?" Questions

1. During Sophie's visit, her nana remembered a very special person who meant a lot to her. Who was that person?

    Aunt Grace

2. What did she think of when she remembered Aunt Grace? Why?

    Mustard seeds and gardenias—they are both small but do great things. A tiny mustard seed grows into a very big plant, and the sweet smell of a tiny gardenia fills up an entire room. In the same way, God uses a small amount of faith to do very big and wonderful things.

3. Sophie's Great Aunt Grace had lived a life of love and faithfulness. Do you think she had won favor and a good name with her family and with God?

   Yes—many years after she died, she was still remembered with respect and admiration because of the way she lived her life.

4. How do you "bind love and faithfulness" around your neck and write them on the tablet of your heart?

   You are writing them on the tablet of your heart each time you learn your memory verse! Ask the Lord to teach you how to love Him more and how to show His love to other people through your words and actions.

Prayer

Memory Verse: "A good name is more desirable than great riches; to be esteemed is better than silver or gold" (Proverbs 22:1, NIV).

Chapter 2 Devotional 3: The Old Pictures

Scripture Reading: "Let love and faithfulness never leave you; bind them around your neck, write them on the tablet of your heart. Then you will win favor and a good name in the sight of God and man" (Proverbs 3:3–4, NIV).

Sophie was visiting her nana, and they had pulled down an old photograph album that Sophie saw sitting on one of the shelves in the bookcase. It was really old, and Sophie just knew there had to be some interesting pictures in it. So she asked her nana if they could look at it together. After Nana pulled it down, they sat together on the couch and began to go through it.

"Whoa, Nana, they are really old, aren't they?" said Sophie.

Nana laughed and said, "Well…yes…they *are* really old! This album belonged to your great-grandmother, and I was just a young girl when these pictures were taken. There are many of these people I never knew—or knew very little about. We moved away not too long after most of these pictures were taken, so there were fewer and fewer pictures of our extended family. However, some of these people I *do* remember, and my mother knew them all and would speak of them occasionally. Look, see this one? This was my great auntie, and she was a sweetheart!"

"What's a great auntie?" asked Sophie.

"A great auntie is the sister of a grandmother," replied Nana.

"Oh, you mean like Auntie Helen?"

"Exactly—so this great auntie was my mother's older sister, but I remember her very well." Nana paused for a moment and then said,

"Auntie Grace was her name, and whenever I remember her, I think of gardenias and mustard seeds."

"Gardenias and mustard seeds!" exclaimed Sophie. "How can you put those together?"

Nana laughed again and said, "I know, it sounds silly, doesn't it? But she loved gardenias and always grew them, and when they were blooming, she would keep just a few in her house. Gardenias have a strong perfume, so you only need a few. She would say her few flowers reminded her of a tiny mustard seed, which grows into a huge plant—and that if you have faith no bigger than a mustard seed, God will do great things with it. So she would put just a few gardenias in her home, but their perfume would fill her whole house." Nana paused again, and then she said, "And she was right, Sophie. God will use our little bit of faith and make something beautiful of it, just like He made a small flower to fill its surroundings with a sweet perfume. When I think of Auntie Grace, it isn't just the gardenias and mustard seeds that I think of—but I am reminded of one of the first people in my life who lived a life of faith and passed that wisdom along to me. And every time I meet someone whose name is Grace, I think of my Auntie Grace."

Sophie was still for a minute and then said, "At home, we've been talking about names and what they mean and how other people think of us when they hear our names. The other day, Mom and I were shopping, and the saleslady told us of someone whose name brought up a bad memory. I'm glad your Auntie Grace gave you a good memory, Nana."

"I am, too!" replied Nana. "You know, probably all of us can think of some bad memories associated with names, but it is God's good grace that supplies many good ones too. He also supplies the grace to help us forgive those who have hurt us. But we do want to live in such a way that when people hear our name, they have pleasant thoughts and memories of us."

"You're right, and I'm glad you told me about your Auntie Grace! This is a sweet picture of her…but Nana?"

"Yes?"

"She really did have funny hair, didn't she?"

What Do You Think?

1. During Sophie's visit, her nana remembered a very special person who meant a lot to her. Who was that person?
2. What did she think of when she remembered Aunt Grace? Why?
3. Sophie's Great Aunt Grace had lived a life of love and faithfulness. Do you think she had won favor and a good name with her family and with God?
4. How do you "bind love and faithfulness" around your neck and write them on the tablet of your heart?

Prayer

Memory Verse: "A good name is more desirable than great riches; to be esteemed is better than silver or gold" (Proverbs 22:1, NIV).

CHAPTER 3:
A Trusting Heart

Parent's Guide for Chapter 3: A Trusting Heart

Emphasis

Sophie struggles with her studies and tells her mom that when she makes a C, "it just makes me feel stupid! And then I get this little knot in my stomach that makes me feel afraid and unimportant." Sophie's mom helps her understand the difference between the "fact" that she is valuable and the "feeling" that makes her think she has little value. She assures Sophie of how much she is loved and of how she is greatly loved and valued by God, who "chose us even before the world was formed to be His sons and daughters."

Memory Verse: "Trust in the Lord with all your heart and lean not on your own understanding; in all your ways submit to Him, and He will make your paths straight" (Proverbs 3:5–6, NIV).

Suggested Answers to "What Do You Think?" Questions

1. In the story, Sophie says she sometimes feels "dumb" or "stupid" when her friends do better in school than she does, and then she feels "afraid and unimportant." Do you ever feel this way?

    Give them time to answer. Most children by age six or seven feel this way from time to time. However, even if they are unable to express it, hearing that other children have these feelings helps them. It is important for your children to know that just because they "feel unimportant" does not make it <u>true</u>!

2. Did you know that feelings come from our emotions and that

God made us with emotions? What are some feelings or emotions?

Happy, sad, excited, lonely, angry, afraid, good/bad mood

*Remind your children that feelings are not good or bad—they just <u>are</u>! How we **respond** to our feelings can be good or bad. For example, calling someone a bad name when we get angry over something they did is never God's way to respond.*

3. In Psalm 139 (NIV), King David said, "You [God] knit me together in my mother's womb." King David also said that God's thoughts about him were too many to count! Since God thinks about all of us that way, do you think we can depend on Him when we are afraid or sad?

Yes. When God says something, it is <u>always true</u>! God said He planned you before you were born and that you are valuable to Him—and that is a <u>fact</u>, not a feeling!

Prayer

Review Memory Verse: "Trust in the Lord with all your heart and lean not on your own understanding; in all your ways submit to Him, and He will make your paths straight" (Proverbs 3:5–6, NIV).

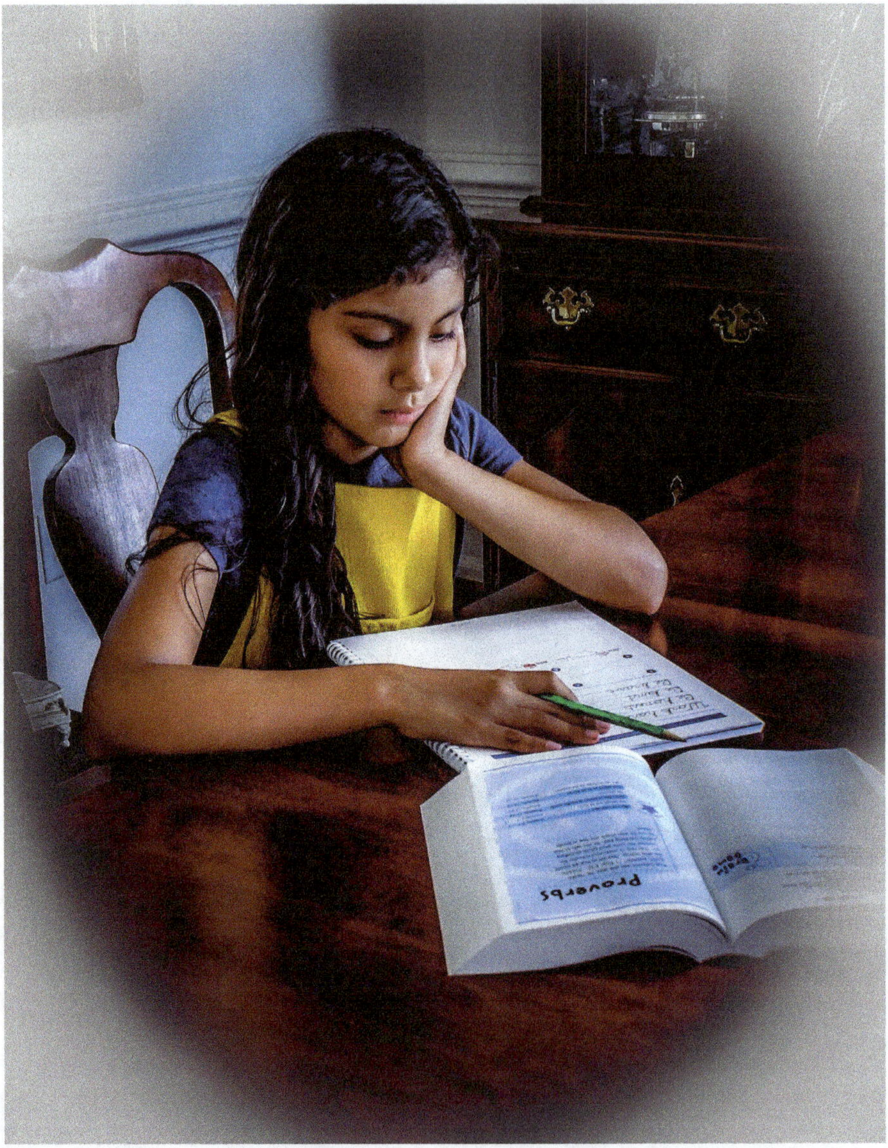
Proverbs

Chapter Three:
A Trusting Heart

Sophie sat wearily at the kitchen table doing her homework. She had been working on it for a long time and was almost through. She had just written the last answer down as her mom came into the kitchen.

"All done, Sophie dear?" said her mother.

"I just finished," Sophie said with a sigh, and a tear trickled down her cheek.

Her mom put her arm around Sophie's shoulders and said, "Is that a tear I see?"—which made the tears *stream* down Sophie's face.

"What's wrong, hon?"

Sophie brushed her tears away and said, "I just feel so dumb sometimes. Ruthie makes As nearly all the time, and she has to tell everybody about it. I make As and Bs and sometimes Cs, and…it just makes me feel stupid! And then I feel afraid and unimportant."

"Unimportant?" her mom said.

"Uh-huh," Sophie replied.

Her mom sat down at the table and looked at her with that "how do I explain this" look.

"Well," she said, "let me see…Ummm…what is your name?"

Sophie giggled and said, "*Mommmm.*"

"Just play along with me, okay?"

"Okay, it's Sophie Anne."

"And who are you, Sophie Anne?"

Sophie thought her mom could be really weird sometimes, but she said, "You know who I am."

"That's true, I do—but do you?"

"Well, of course, I do—I'm your daughter, and Dad's daughter, and Elizabeth's sister, and Nana and Papa's granddaughter, and I'm in the fifth grade at school, and I'm an American, and…and…and…I'm God's daughter, too!"

Her mom laughed and said, "That is so, so true—and so much more. And you bring us all great joy! Now, let me read you something that I found many years ago, and it still fills me with wonder every time I read it." (Sophie again thought about how sometimes her mom just talks a little strangely.)

Her mom picked up the Bible that was on the sideboard and said, "These are some verses in Psalm 139:

> For you created my inmost being; You knit me together in my mother's womb. I praise You because I am fearfully and wonderfully made; Your works are wonderful, I know that full well. How precious to me are Your thoughts, God! How vast is the sum of them.
>
> Psalm 139:13, 14, 17 (NIV)

You know, Sophie, maybe the psalmist David wrote this psalm because he was experiencing some of the same feelings you have tonight. He tried very hard to serve his king, and yet King Saul was very jealous of him. Do you remember this story?"

"I think so," replied Sophie. "Wasn't this the one where he had to hide from the king?"

"Yes, it was. The king knew David was greatly loved by the people, and he thought David wanted his throne, so he made life very hard for David. King Saul even wanted David killed! And David often had to hide from him and sometimes even hid in caves. But David knew he belonged to God and that no matter where he was, God was there also. Yet there were times when he felt really fearful and alone."

"Kind of like I do tonight?" said Sophie.

"And I'm so sorry you're feeling that way," said her mom as she put her arm around her. "But just like David knew the truth, I want you to know the truth—that God can see us in the night hours just as well as He can see us in the day hours. Darkness and light are just the same to God. And you know, the truth of the matter is that *truth* is what God says it is—and that never changes! Feelings, however, do change. Feelings are a wonderful part of us. To be able to feel loved, to feel we belong, and to feel joy and happiness—these are all wonderful expressions of life that God created for us to enjoy. But we also feel afraid sometimes, lonely, or sad, don't we? We don't have any problem with the good feelings of love or being happy, but we can surely get troubled over the scary ones. Now, let's get back to what you said about how you feel afraid and unimportant—wasn't that what you said?"

"Uh-huh, I do feel that way sometimes," Sophie said.

"And what was it you said about who you are?" said her mom.

"Well, that I'm a daughter, and a sister, and a granddaughter, and God's daughter," replied Sophie.

"And I said, 'that is so true,' and that is what we always come back to, what and who is the truth! That you are my little girl is an absolute fact. It isn't a feeling; nothing you can feel or do or say will ever change that. Are you valuable and important to me?"

"Of course I am—you're my mother!" exclaimed Sophie.

"Yes, because that is the truth! Sometimes you may get upset or angry over something I have done and feel like I don't love you—or that what you think isn't important to me. Does that ever happen?" asked her mom.

Sophie sighed and said, "*Mommm*, how do you know that?"

"Because I was a young lady too, and I can remember thinking *if she loved me, she would let me do whatever I wanted to do!* Do you think Nana didn't love me when that happened?"

"No…Nana always loved you just like she will always love us!" replied Sophie.

"Exactly!" replied her mom. "And occasionally, you may have an angry or upset feeling, but just like Nana, the way you feel doesn't change the fact of how much I love you or that you are very, very valuable and important to me! Now…if you are that valuable to me, just think how enormously valuable you are to God—because He chose you even before the world was formed to be His daughter."

"Really?" said Sophie.

"Yes, really! There are times in all of our lives when, if we go by just our feelings, we might be afraid or think that we aren't very important to God or anyone else. But always remember, it isn't what we feel about ourselves that we depend on—it's who we are and, most importantly, *who* we belong to that is important. And we belong to Christ, and Christ belongs to God, so that puts us in pretty special company. *And those are the facts!* Remember, facts are like the engine of a train, and feelings are like the caboose. There may be a hundred cars between the engine and the caboose, but eventually, the caboose comes along. So the next time you feel afraid and unimportant, perhaps you can stop where you are and ask the Lord to help you remember the *fact* of how important you are to Him, and to me, and to your dad, and to your sister, and to your nana and papa, and to your cousins, and to your friends, and…"

Sophie giggled and said, "Okay, okay, okay…"

When Sophie went to bed that night, her mom came in and prayed for her. She asked the Lord to help Sophie know more and more about the *fact* of belonging to Him. Sophie drifted off to sleep, thinking, *I guess the engine is working because I feel really safe and warm.*

What Do You Think?

1. In the story, Sophie says she sometimes feels "dumb" or "stupid" when her friends do better in school than she does, and then she feels "afraid and unimportant." Do you ever feel this way?
2. Did you know that feelings come from our emotions and that God made us with emotions? What are some feelings or emotions?
3. In Psalm 139 (NIV), King David said, "You [God] knit me together in my mother's womb" (in his mommy's tummy). King David also said that God's thoughts about him were too many to count! Since God thinks about all of us that way, do you think we can depend on Him when we are afraid or sad?

Prayer

Review Memory Verse: "Trust in the Lord with all your heart and lean not on your own understanding; in all your ways submit to Him, and He will make your paths straight" (Proverbs 3:5–6, NIV).

SUPPLY LIST FOR ACTIVITY 3

Collections: pictures of each child (baby, dedication/baptism, school, birthday party, holidays, vacations, family, etc.)

* * *

Activity 3

The activity for this lesson is designed to give the parent(s) private time with each child in order to see if there is anything in particular that is troubling him or her.

Start with a collection of pictures of each child, *i.e.*, baby, dedication or baptism, school, birthday party, Christmas and other holidays, and vacation or family pictures. The emphasis will be to show each child's individuality while showing that each child is part of a family—unique and special. Spread the child's pictures on the dining room table or on the living room floor in age progression to present an overall representation of the child's years. Then talk about the different events. The ones the child does not remember can be a special time as he or she realizes how important he/she is to you. Special honors (school, grades, sports, dance, etc.) can also be mentioned. During this discussion, remind your child of different times when you knew the Lord was leading you a certain way or when you knew prayers for this child had been answered. Ask the Lord's direction so your child will know that we all have issues for which we need prayer. Then when the time is right (and it may be later on in the week after your child has had time to think or has the courage to tell you), talk to your child to see if anything is troubling him or her. Problems may be in reference to the memory verse for the week, regarding your child's understanding of a certain situation, or just regarding his/her own fears or insecurities. Nothing is too small or insignificant. Very young children may be upset because they have a "boo-boo" that hurts, but they can learn at an early age that anything can be brought to the Father in prayer. And if you find your child is really troubled about something, please don't feel like you must have all the answers to the problem. Just give assurance that you will try to find answers and that you will continually be there praying for and available to him or her—ever trusting that God is working and will continue to work in his or her life.

This experience may not produce any revelations for you, and you may feel nothing was accomplished. But never fear—children will remember this for a long time! If you continue to remind them by your words and actions that you are there for them, the time will come when they will confide in you. Just don't take too long because the older they get without this kind of relationship, the harder it will be to establish.

Parent's Guide for Chapter 3 Devotional 1: Trusting in the Lord

Emphasis

To understand what it means to trust and that our ability to trust is based on the reliability of the person or object we are trusting.

Scripture Reading: "Whoever fears the Lord has a secure fortress, and for their children it will be a refuge" (Proverbs 14:26, NIV).

Suggested Answers to "What Do You Think?" Questions

1. Let's think about what you trust. Why do you think the chair you are sitting in will hold you up? Why do you think the ice cream in your freezer will stay frozen?

    The chair is made of strong wood (or metal). Electricity keeps the freezer working.

2. Now let's think about who you trust. Why do you think you will get a birthday present on your birthday? Who is the strongest power in heaven or in the entire world? Who is like a strong castle where we can go and always be safe?

    Your mom and/or dad love you and want to give you good things—like a present on your birthday.

3. Fill in the blanks: The chair is made of strong wood and always holds you up, so you can *trust* it. The freezer is connected to a strong source of electricity that keeps the temperature freezing, so you can *trust* that the ice cream will be frozen. You always have a birthday gift on your birthday because you can *trust* that your mom and/or dad love you and love giving you good things. God is the strongest power in heaven or in the entire world and is like a strong castle where we can go and always be safe—and therefore, you can trust God with everything in your life! This is *not* a feeling—it is an absolute *fact*!

Prayer

Review Memory Verse: "Trust in the Lord with all your heart and lean not on your own understanding; in all your ways submit to him, and He will make your paths straight" (Proverbs 3:5–6, NIV).

Chapter 3 Devotional 1: Trusting in the Lord

Scripture Reading: "Whoever fears the Lord has a secure fortress, and for their children it will be a refuge" (Proverbs 14:26, NIV).

Sophie had just finished breakfast and was reciting her memory verse for the week to her mom. "Trust in the Lord with all your heart and…" She paused and said, "I was just wondering…What does it mean to 'trust in the Lord with all your heart'?"

"Well," said Sophie's mom, "What do you think it means to trust someone?"

"I guess it means that I think they will be my friend and try not to do anything that will hurt me or hurt my feelings," replied Sophie. "I trust Elizabeth, although sometimes she doesn't really act like my friend—but I know she loves me even when we disagree and argue with each other. And I have friends like Hannah and Mary Sue and Jackson, who are really nice to me; and when I need help with something, they are always glad to help me if they can. And I guess I trust my teacher because I think she really tries to be a good teacher, and I trust our pastor because he and his wife are really interested in all of us, and…"

"That's all true, Sophie, but what about your dear old mom?"

"*Mommmm!*" cried Sophie, "of course I trust you—you're my *mother*! You are always here. You're like Nana and Papa and Uncle Mike and Aunt Kikky, who are always around and who love me like you do, and like Dad, who lives a long way away—but I can always call him!"

"I know, and I was just teasing, but why is it that you so easily say you trust us?"

"Because I know you all love me, and we are family, and because…

well…you always listen to me when I am upset about something, and you let me visit my friends and have them over, and you work hard so I can have things, and…and…well, you're just a good mom!"

"And," replied her mom, "just like you trust us, you can trust the Lord! Trust, Sophie, is the firm belief in the reliability, truth, and strength of the one you are trusting. When we trust people, it means we really, really believe that they want only what is true and right for themselves and for those around them, so anything they do for us and for those we love will always be for our best. There is no greater strength in the entire universe than the strength of the Lord. Way back at the beginning of recorded biblical history, trust was something the Jewish people gave to God because they understood that He was so very big and powerful and that His faithfulness would last forever."

"That's right," said Sophie. "He even parted the waters for Moses and the people, didn't He?"

"Yes, it was His strength that they relied on time after time. David, the great king, said in one of the psalms, 'Some trust in chariots and some trust in horses, but we trust in the name of the Lord, our God' [Psalm 20:7, NIV]. Today that would be like saying, 'America may trust in a strong Army and Navy, and many may trust in how much money they have, but we will put our trust in the mighty name of the Lord; for because of *His* strength and *His* love, He will always do what is best for us.' So today, let's ask the Lord to help us know that we can always trust Him, and tomorrow perhaps we can talk about the 'with all your heart.'"

"Okay…and Mom?"

"Yes?"

"I love you," replied Sophie.

"And I love you too, dear, dear Sophie."

(*I've said it before,* Sophie thought, *she will still be saying that when I am really old—at twenty-five or even thirty.*)

What Do You Think?

1. Let's think about *what* you trust. Why do you think the chair you are sitting in will hold you up? Why do you think the ice cream in your freezer will stay frozen?
2. Now let's think about *who* you trust. Why do you think you will get a birthday present on your birthday? Who is the strongest power in heaven or in the entire world? Who is like a strong castle where we can go and always be safe?
3. Fill in the blanks: The chair is made of strong wood and always holds you up so you can _____ it. The freezer is connected to a strong source of electricity that keeps the temperature freezing so you can _____ that the ice cream will be frozen. You always have a birthday gift on your birthday because you can _____ that your mom and/or dad love you and love giving you good things. God is the strongest power in heaven or in the entire world and is like a strong castle where we can go and always be safe—and therefore, you can _____ God with everything in your life! This is *not* a feeling—it is an absolute _____!
4. And remember: "Whoever fears the Lord has a secure fortress, and for their children it will be a refuge" (Proverbs 14:26, NIV).

Review Memory Verse: "Trust in the Lord with all your heart and lean not on your own understanding; in all your ways submit to Him, and He will make your paths straight" (Proverbs 3:5–6, NIV).

Parent's Guide for Chapter 3 Devotional 2: United Attention

Emphasis

To help children understand that the heart reflects who we are in our thoughts, our emotions, and our actions and that the Lord longs for our hearts to be united in these ways. In this particular devotional, you can easily draw a heart on red construction paper and then cut it out. Divide the heart into three parts and write one of the following words on each part: Mind, Feelings, Choices. This will help your child see how our hearts can be either divided or united. Examples can also be written on each part, *i.e.*, Mind—all the things we think of; Feelings—love, joy, anger; Choices—the things we do.

Scripture Reading and Memory Verse: "Trust in the Lord with all your heart and lean not on your own understanding; in all your ways submit to Him, and He will make your paths straight" (Proverbs 3:5–6, NIV).

Suggested Answers to "What Do You Think?" Questions

1. On this particular night, Sophie was so happy because the party she and her friends helped plan had been a big success. Her teacher had told them how proud she was of them because they had worked "with all their hearts" on it. What had Sophie and her friends done to make her teacher say that?

    They wanted to have a party that everyone would enjoy—even the quiet and shy ones. Sophie and her friends had all helped plan the details of the party. During the party, everyone was included in all the activities.

2. Sophie's mom tells her about another psalm that asks the Lord to "unite my heart to fear Your name; I will give thanks to You with all my heart." If you know you should do something because it is the right thing to do, but you choose to do something else, can you say you are doing it "with all your heart"?

(The scripture reference is found in Psalm 86:11–12, NASB)

No—because your heart is divided! Your mind, feelings, and choices have to work together in order for you to have an "undivided" heart. Only when you have an undivided heart can you love and trust God with <u>all</u> your heart.

3. Read your scripture reading (memory verse) again. What do you think it means? to lean not on your own understanding? And to acknowledge Him in all your ways? And that God will make our paths straight?

You will not always understand why things happen the way they do. Honor God by choosing to follow Jesus' example of how to live and how to treat other people. God has promised to always be with you and to go before you in everything you do.

Chapter 3 Devotional 2: United Attention

Sophie had just crawled into bed for the night when her mom came in and sat down on the bed beside her.

"Did you have a good time at the party this evening?" asked her mom.

"Oh, it was great! The food was good, we played games, we got to do karaoke, and I made some new friends. It was a fun, fun party, and after a while, even the shy ones joined in. I was so happy that I got to help plan the party. We all worked so hard to plan things so everyone could join in the fun."

"I think you all did a wonderful job planning and putting it all together. I know the teachers who were in charge were very appreciative of all you did," said her mom.

"Yes, I think so. After the party, Mrs. Morgan told me that she was very proud of all of us who worked on it. She said it was because we worked *with all our hearts* to make it special. Mom! That's like our scripture verse this week—you know, 'Trust in the Lord with all your heart.' Is that what it means?"

"I think that is a wonderful illustration! There is a psalm that says, 'unite my heart to fear Your name; I will give thanks to You with all my heart.' At first, we think, *Well, I just have one heart—how do I unite it?* But what we do and what we think comes out of our hearts, and it is easy to be divided when we know one thing but choose to do another. So when our minds, and our feelings, and our choices all work together, then we have an undivided heart, and we will be able to 'trust Him with all our heart'—which He thinks is very special."

"I think I understand...but you *do* remember that I'm only ten!"

Sophie's mom laughed and gave her a big hug. "I know...but that's one of the great things about our Lord—*He* is the one we can trust to help us understand."

Sophie's mom prayed a *goodnight* prayer and thanked the Lord for bringing Sophie into her life. Then she asked Him to bless Sophie and continue to help her see how very special she is to Him and how much He loves to help His children understand all about His ways.

Scripture Reading and Memory Verse: "Trust in the Lord with all your heart and lean not on your own understanding; in all your ways submit to Him, and He will make your paths straight" (Proverbs 3:5–6, NIV).

What Do You Think?

1. On this particular night, Sophie was so happy because the party she and her friends helped plan had been a great success. Her teacher had told them how proud she was of them because they had worked "with all their hearts" on it. What had Sophie and her friends done to make her teacher say that?

2. Sophie's mom tells her of another psalm that says, "unite my heart to fear Your name; I will give thanks to You with all my heart." If you know you should do something because it is right—but you choose to do something else, are you doing it with "all your heart"?

3. Read your scripture reading (memory verse) again. What do you think it means?
   - We may not always understand why things happen as they do.
   - But we make choices to follow Jesus' example of how to love other people.
   - And we know God has promised to be with us and will go be-

fore us in all that we do.

Prayer

Review Memory Verse: "Trust in the Lord with all your heart and lean not on your own understanding; in all your ways submit to Him, and He will make your paths straight" (Proverbs 3:5–6, NIV).

Parent's Guide for Chapter 3
Devotional 3:
Elizabeth's Friend

Emphasis

To help children see the need for praying for people who are going through difficult circumstances and that even when we do not understand why some things happen, we can trust in the sovereignty of God.

Scripture Reading: "For the Lord gives wisdom; from His mouth come knowledge and understanding. He holds success in store for the upright; He is a shield to those whose walk is blameless, for He guards the course of the just and protects the way of His faithful ones" (Proverbs 2:6–8, NIV).

Suggested Answers to "What Do You Think?" Questions

1. According to your scripture reading, who gives wisdom, knowledge, and understanding?

   The Lord

2. Your scripture also says that God gives victory to those who walk with Him and that He will guard and protect those who are faithful to Him…but sometimes, things happen that we just don't understand. Do you know someone who is sick, or a family who needs help, or perhaps someone who is out of work

and needs a job?

Give children time to answer and express their concerns. While we never want to overwhelm our children with needs they cannot possibly understand, they usually know about friends or relatives who are sick or have other needs.

3. When tough things happen to our friends or to us, what can we do?

    Pray for them and ask God to supply what they need. Remember to trust God because He knows and understands so much more than we do. When God answers your prayer, remember to thank Him for His faithfulness.

Prayer

Memory Verse: "Trust in the Lord with all your heart and lean not on your own understanding; in all your ways submit to Him, and He will make your paths straight" (Proverbs 3:5–6, NIV).

Chapter 3 Devotional 3: Elizabeth's Friend

Scripture Reading: "For the Lord gives wisdom, from His mouth comes knowledge and understanding. He holds success in store for the upright; He is a shield to those whose walk is blameless, for He guards the course of the just and protects the way of His faithful ones" (Proverbs 2:6–8, NIV).

Sophie, Elizabeth, and their mom were talking about the day's events while eating dinner on Friday evening. Elizabeth had just finished telling her about a friend at school whose brother had been in a car accident and had broken his arm. He was a great basketball player, and now he wouldn't be able to play for the rest of the season. This was a real disappointment because he was a senior and was hoping to get a scholarship for college.

"It's really tough for him, Mom," said Elizabeth. "His chances of getting a scholarship were very good, and now it looks like there is no way that can ever happen. It's hard to understand! He's such a neat guy; his grades are good, he's president of the Community Get Involved Club, and now he will sit on the sidelines at the games, and his plans for college are just not going to happen—*and*...he's a believer! Trusting that everything will work out is just not that easy, is it?"

"I'm sorry to hear about your friend, and you're right; it isn't easy to trust the Lord when life doesn't work out the way you think it should. Because I'm your mom and would like to make your lives as easy as possible, sometimes I wish I had answers for you that didn't require trusting. But then I would be playing *God*, wouldn't I?"

"Well," said Sophie slowly in a soft whisper, "I don't mean to be disrespectful—but we all know you aren't God, don't we?"

Elizabeth and their mom turned and looked at Sophie, and both of them started laughing. "You're absolutely right!" said their mom. "We all know that I am certainly not God, and now that we have that completely understood, let's look again at our verse for the week."

So Elizabeth, Sophie, and their mom quoted the verse together, "Trust in the Lord with all your heart and lean not on your own understanding; in all your ways submit to Him, and He will make your paths straight."

"You see," said their mom, "if we had to rely only on *our* understanding, we would all be overwhelmed by things that happen in life. The promise is that when we trust *God*'s understanding and acknowledge that *He* is God and absolutely and lovingly in control of our lives, *He* is the one who will make life *right*! Later, when we look back on our circumstances, we will understand. Of course, that is easier said than done, so we must continue to ask Him to increase our understanding of what 'trusting' means. So let's continue to pray for your friend, Elizabeth, and do our part in trusting the Lord for his healing and for his ability to trust the Lord."

What Do You Think?

1. According to your scripture reading, who gives wisdom, knowledge, and understanding?
2. Your scripture reading also says that God gives victory to those who walk with Him and that He will guard and protect those who are faithful to Him…but sometimes, things happen that we just don't understand. Do you know someone who is sick, a family who needs help, or someone who is out of work and needs a job?
3. When tough things happen to our friends or to us, what can we do?

Prayer

Memory Verse: "Trust in the Lord with all your heart and lean not on your own understanding; in all your ways submit to Him, and He will make your paths straight" (Proverbs 3:5–6, NIV).

CHAPTER 4: Sophie Speaks about Good Friends

Parent's Guide for Chapter 4: Sophie Speaks about Good Friends

Emphasis

Chapter 4 introduces Jackson, Sophie's cousin, who is also a good friend, and Uncle Mike and Aunt Kikky—all of whom live next door and are great supporters of Sophie, Elizabeth, and their mom. Sophie explains why Jackson is such a good friend, which reveals the purpose of the chapter: the value of being a good friend and the value of having good friends.

Memory Verse: "Oil and perfume make the heart glad. And a person's advice is sweet to his friend" (Proverbs 27:9, NASB).

Suggested Answers to "What Do You Think?" Questions

1. Do you have a good friend like Jackson?

2. What do you especially like about your friends?

    Fun to be with, interested in the same things you are, easy to talk to and share with, etc.

3. If one of your friends told you his or her parents were getting a divorce, would knowing about Jackson's life help you understand how to be a good friend to them?

    He <u>listened</u> to her! He also told her he was sorry, he did not embarrass her when she started to cry, and he showed he cared about her by telling her it was good to have a best friend.

4. What was the best thing Sophie liked about Jackson?

   She could trust him.

Prayer

Ask God to help you be the kind of friend who comforts those who are hurting.

Memory Verse: "Oil and perfume make the heart glad, and a person's advice is sweet to his friend" (Proverbs 27:9, NASB).

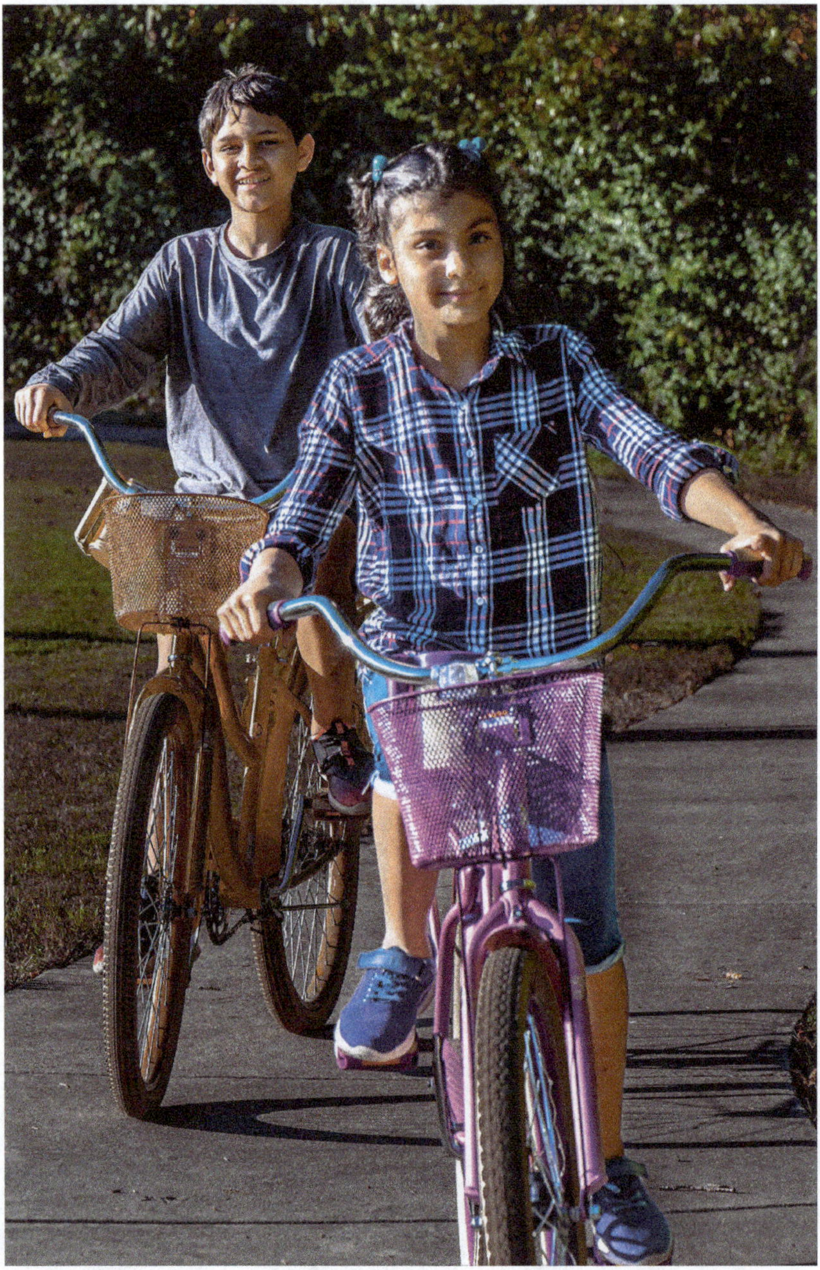

Chapter Four:
Sophie Speaks about Good Friends

Jackson is a very, very special friend of mine...because Jackson is also my *cousin*! Calling my cousin a really good friend may sound unusual—after all, you can have many cousins, but that just means you are related to them. But sometimes they make good friends, and that's what Jackson is! When we hang out together, some people make the mistake of thinking he is my boyfriend. But Jackson is my *friend*—who just happens to be a boy!

People can be really ridiculous about girlfriends and boyfriends—like my sister and her girlfriends. They can talk about boys for hours and hours—in front of anyone—and not even be embarrassed: "He is *soooooo* cute...did you know he's getting a football scholarship? He winked at me when I walked by him at the restaurant..." You'd think they could find something better to talk about.

So, let me tell you about Jackson. He is ten years old and is in my class at school, and we moved into the house next door to him about two years ago. His dad is my mom's brother, which makes him my uncle. Uncle Mike and his wife, Aunt Kikky, are lots of fun, and I love them very much. Jackson is the youngest kid in their family. He has one older brother and two older sisters, so he *understands* perfectly about sisters and their boyfriends. One sister is already married and lives across town; his brother is in college, and his other sister lives at home. She is the same age as Elizabeth.

Aunt Kikky says Jackson was their special surprise—whatever that means—but I think it has something to do with the fact that they are kind of old to have a ten-year-old child. In fact, they are *really* old—I think like fifty and fifty-one—so it's a little amazing that they still understand kids fairly well. But let's get back to Jackson. We discuss our problems with sisters and the whole thing about boyfriends and girlfriends from time to time…but not too often because it just isn't very important. What *is* important is that Jackson is a good friend! When I was learning how to ride a bike, he *never* laughed at me. He would see me wobble and fall and would just say, "You'll get it soon; I used to fall all the time too." Or, when I would have problems with fractions in math, he would say, "Maybe I can help you with it after school." But he *really* was my friend when the big *divorce* happened with my parents. It still makes me really sad, and I will talk about it later; but when I told Jackson, he just looked at me and said, "I'm sorry, Sophie, that must be really hard." When I told him, I tried not to let any tears come out, but it's really hard because your throat hurts, and that just makes it worse…so some did come out, and he just pretended not to see, and we rode bikes for a while. But before he went into his house, he looked at me and said, "I'm glad we're friends—it's good to have a best friend!"

When I went to bed that night, I told Mom about it. I didn't know it would make her cry. She had really big tears in her eyes, and she said, "I'm sorry also, and I'm glad you have good friends too." Then we prayed about my day, and I felt better. I always feel better when my mom prays for me, and I haven't figured that out yet. I think it has something to do with the **Ho-ly Spir-it,** but that's another *big subject*, and right now, I want to talk about Jackson.

So anyway, Jackson is a good friend, though you must realize he *is* still a boy…*and*…we are very different about many things. For instance, he has a really hard time being still. Sometimes he comes over to play *Monopoly*, and he gets up to get a drink, and then he rocks his chair back and forth, and then he walks around the table, and his money and property cards are all over the place. I'm surprised that he can keep up with where he is in the game, but he seems to handle it well and wins as often as I do. So I have decided it is just a "boy thing"! Another "boy thing" is the way he digs up worms. He actually *enjoys it!* He does it when he and his dad go fishing, so I guess it's necessary—but he thinks it's great fun. He puts them in a jar with a little bit of dirt, and then he wants to show them to me like he just found a one-hundred-dollar bill! He is *so* proud of them! So I *try* to act like they are great…it is *really* hard! But since he is my friend, I tell him he did a good job and that I hope they catch many, many fish. Sometimes when they go fishing, Uncle Mike asks me to go along. He promises to get the fishing pole all ready for me, so all I have to do is hang it over the side of the boat. I do have to say that being out on the water with them is a fun thing. Uncle Mike is fun and funny, and we have some good talks about school and friends.

There are other things, though, that Jackson and I do together. He likes to read, and I do too. He likes mysteries and stories about brave men and women, and so do I. He will tell me about the ones he reads, and I will tell him about the ones I read—and we wonder if we could ever be that brave or courageous. I tell him that he, of course, would be, and then he tells me that I, of course, would also be very brave. Sometimes he and his sister come over so she and Elizabeth Grace can "babysit" us while his parents and my mom go out for the evening. That is when we talk about all these things. We also play computer games together. He's very good at these, and we just have fun.

I guess the best thing I like about Jackson, though, is that I know I can trust him. If I tell him someone hurt my feelings, he doesn't go around blabbing it to everyone. He will talk to me about it and even tell me if he thinks I may have misunderstood what the problem was. But he doesn't make fun of me, and if I ask him to keep it a secret, I know he will. I hope I can always be as good a friend to Jackson as he is to me. I have other good friends too—like Mary Sue and Hannah—but I'm glad I have Jackson…who is not only my cousin but my friend!

Memory Verse: "Oil and perfume make the heart glad, and a person's advice is sweet to his friend" (Proverbs 27:9, NASB).

What Do You Think?

1. Do you have a good friend like Jackson?
2. What do you especially like about your friends?
3. If one of your friends told you his or her parents were getting a divorce, would knowing about Jackson's life help you know how to help your friend?
4. What was the best thing Sophie liked about Jackson?

Prayer

Memory Verse: "Oil and perfume make the heart glad, and a person's advice is sweet to his friend" (Proverbs 27:9, NASB).

SUPPLY LIST FOR ACTIVITY 4

Have a special event for close friends (event suggestions following the chapter). Write special cards to invited friends or make them with colored computer paper with leftover stickers from Chapter 2.

***

Activity 4

This activity is designed to acknowledge and honor your child's friends in a social gathering. If you have more than one child, a social event could be planned for each child and his or her friends. (If two of your children are close in age, you could have one big event to celebrate all of their friends.) This kind of activity can be challenging for a single parent. If you are a single mom and have both a son and a daughter, you could ask an uncle or grandfather to help with your son's activities. If you are a single dad with both a son and a daughter, you could ask an aunt or grandmother to help with your daughter's activities. You may even have good friends who would be willing to help you. The important thing is that you want your son or daughter to be comfortable with whoever helps you.

Have family time together to discuss the event. Let them know that this social event is to honor and celebrate their respective friends and discuss what they would like to do. Keep in mind that it can be a small outing (hamburgers and fries at McDonald's or a dessert time one evening). Some of their ideas may be expensive, so set your budget and let them know they must stay within that budget or contribute some of their own money. Following are just a few ideas to get you started:

1. Plan a "dinner-over" evening, serving something simple like spaghetti or hamburgers, followed by table games. Make a "friends' cake" with a candle for each friend (much like a birthday cake) as a grand finale. Select a party favor for each friend to take home.

2. Pick up your child's friends for an early hamburger dinner at a fast-food restaurant or for pizza. Bring the party favors and the "friends' cake" to the restaurant for dessert.

3. Invite your child's friends to your home for a Saturday morning pancake breakfast, and then have a fun event for them after breakfast. Make a "monkey bread cake" for your "friends' cake" and serve it after the event before they go home.

Event Suggestions for Girls
- Ask your daughter's friends to bring their favorite "Barbie Doll" and have a "Barbie-Get-Acquainted" time.
- Provide a dance exercise video where they can let loose their energy. (Mom must participate.)
- Provide manicures and/or pedicures for all the girls. Ask sever-

al of your friends to help you with this project.

Event Suggestions for Boys
- Invite a guest "teacher" to come and give tips on basketball, soccer, football, or golf, giving each boy a chance to participate with him in the examples.

- Organize a game in any of the sports with you as the referee.

- Take them to a Little League baseball, soccer, or football game. Use "monkey bread" for their "friends' cake" and serve it, along with their favors, before leaving for the game.

Then select a date for the event or events and make invitations to send in the mail. Invitations could say, "We are having a Friends' Day Celebration just for YOU! Please come and join the fun." Be sure to include an R.S.V.P. and your phone number. Make sure the date and time are very visible and give a hint about what you will be doing. Mail the invitations at least two to three weeks before the event date. Children will probably have two, three, or four friends they would consider the kind of friends discussed in the story.

At some time before the party, have your child make a special "Thank You" card for each friend, telling each one how much they appreciate their friendship. These can be given out during the "friends' cake" dessert time. Make sure everyone knows that the candles represent the special friends who are there and that you, as a parent, appreciate the friendships your child has. A simple party favor can be given to each friend to take home.

Whatever you choose to do, be it very simple or with much preparation, be assured that your child and the friends will remember this very special "friends' day" for many years to come.

Parent's Guide for Chapter 4 Devotional 1: What Is a Good Friend?

Emphasis

To help children begin to evaluate the friends they have and to see how special it is to have those to whom they can entrust their thoughts, ideas, and problems. It usually takes time to develop this kind of friend, but often their ideas or advice will help us make wise decisions.

Scripture Reading: "The one who gets wisdom loves life; the one who cherishes understanding will soon prosper" (Proverbs 19:8, NIV).

Suggested Answers to "What Do You Think?" Questions

1. Jackson had different kinds of friends. Do you have different kinds of friends? What different kinds do you have?

   Acquaintances, church friends, school friends, activity friends (like soccer, dance class, gymnastics, etc.), neighborhood friends

2. Jackson tells his dad that the friends he thought he could talk to about a problem were the ones he had known for a long time. What was his dad's response?

   When you can take advice from a friend, it is because you trust them—and trust usually takes a long time.

3. Jackson is beginning to understand! How did he explain what a good friend's help was like?

   Like walking into the house and smelling chocolate cookies—or maybe grilled fish and French fries

Prayer

Review Memory Verse: "Oil and perfume make the heart glad, and a person's advice is sweet to his friend" (Proverbs 27:9, NASB).

Chapter 4 Devotional 1: What Is a Good Friend?

Scripture Reading: "The one who gets wisdom loves life; the one who cherishes understanding will soon prosper" (Proverbs 19:8, NIV).

"Dad," said Jackson, "what do you think a good friend is?"

"Well," said Jackson's dad, "that is a subject that requires a bit of thought."

"I know, Dad," replied Jackson. "But you know what I mean. I have many friends—school friends, church friends, and family friends. Some of them I spend more time with than others, but I think they are all my friends. I guess I just know some of them better than I know others."

"You're right, and that is all true. A good friend is a great subject to talk about, and I can't think of a better time than today while we are out here on the lake fishing—and the fish seem to be sleeping! So…is there a particular reason you brought this up?"

"Yes," replied Jackson. "Aunt Cyndi has been talking to Sophie and Elizabeth Grace about things in the Book of Proverbs, and this week they have to memorize a verse about friendship. It's something about good friends being like a sweet perfume. I want to be a good friend, but I do *not* want to smell like sweet perfume!"

Jackson's dad looked at him and laughed! "You have that right, Jackson!" he said. "I want to be a good friend, too—but I *surely* do *not* want to smell like sweet perfume either!"

"Okay," said Jackson, "so what does it mean?"

"Well, first, let's get the quote right. I think it goes something like this,

'When a good friend gives you wise advice, it is as sweet as perfume'—and it *is* a great verse! Perhaps I can explain it this way: when a good friend (someone you trust) gives you his advice about something—and you know it is good advice—it is sort of like walking into the house, smelling freshly baked chocolate chip cookies, and knowing they are for you."

"Wow! Okay, that is much better!" said Jackson. He sat silent for a moment and then looked at his dad. "I guess then…maybe there are different kinds of friends…because most of my friends and I just goof around—you know, play ball and stuff. I enjoy being with them, but we don't talk about much that I would want advice on. I do think they are good friends, though…it's a little confusing."

"Yes, it can be confusing. I think we all have different friends that we enjoy, perhaps because we have things in common; for you, it would be school activities, church activities, and family get-togethers. So since you are involved in doing these things with kids you know you are comfortable with them and enjoy being with them. But do you have a few friends that you could talk to if you were troubled about something?"

"Yes, I have a few, but they are friends that I have known for a long time, and we have hung out together a lot," said Jackson.

"Well, perhaps that is one piece of the puzzle. When you are able to take advice from someone, it is because you trust them—and trust usually happens over time."

"Yes, I understand because I can talk to most of them about almost anything. Maybe a good friend's help is like walking into the house and smelling chocolate chip cookies, or maybe grilled fish and French fries."

"That is a great thought," said Jackson's dad. "However, we better get busy, or there will be no fish to…"

"Oh! Look, Dad," Jackson interrupted, "I think I have a fish on my line!"

"I believe you do," said his dad. "We still have time to catch enough for dinner tonight. We'll talk again soon about friends."

"Okay—he's a big one…you may need to help me."

What Do You Think?

1. Jackson had different kinds of friends. Do you have different kinds of friends? What different kinds do you have?
2. Jackson tells his dad that the friends he thought he could talk to about a problem were the ones he had known for a long time. What was his dad's response?
3. Jackson is beginning to understand! How did he explain what a good friend's help was like?

Prayer

Review Memory Verse: "Oil and perfume make the heart glad, and a person's advice is sweet to his friend" (Proverbs 27:9, NASB).

Parent's Guide for Chapter 4 Devotional 2: Sophie's New Friend

Emphasis

To help children see that friendship is not only about having a good friend—it is also about being a good friend!

Scripture Reading: "One who has unreliable friends soon comes to ruin, but there is a friend who sticks closer than a brother" (Proverbs 18:24, NIV).

Suggested Answers to "What Do You Think?" Questions

1. Sophie noticed something different about her new friend. What did she notice?

   Her friend wanted to know all about Sophie—about her family, about things Sophie enjoyed doing, about what she liked. She didn't just talk about herself and what she liked to do.

2. Sophie learned one of the best things she could do to have a good friend. What did Sophie learn?

   To be interested in the happiness of others.

3. Do you have friends who are like Rachel? Are you a friend like Rachel?

   Encourage your children to be the kind of friends to others that they would like to have themselves.

Prayer

To have good friends like Rachel—and to *be* a good friend like Rachel.

Review Memory Verse: "Oil and perfume make the heart glad, and a person's advice is sweet to his friend" (Proverbs 27:9, NASB).

Chapter 4 Devotional 2: Sophie's New Friend

Scripture Reading: "One who has unreliable friends soon comes to ruin, but there is a friend who sticks closer than a brother" (Proverbs 18:24, NIV).

"I think I have a new friend, Mom," Sophie said at the dinner table one night.

"Really?" replied her mom. "Someone at school?"

"Yes, she's a new girl who's just moved here from Texas."

"She and her family have made a big move then, haven't they?"

"Yes, she said it took two days for them to get here. I think they've moved into a house not too far from us; she lives on Trenton Street. Isn't that the street we were on the other day when we were taking dinner to Mrs. Brown?"

"Yes, it is," replied Sophie's mom. "You're right; that's only a few minutes away from us. Tell me about her."

"Well," said Sophie, "her name is Rachel, and Mrs. Chandler asked me to show her around when we went to lunch—so I showed her the auditorium, the gym, and the lunchroom. Then we had lunch together. She told me they had moved because her dad was transferred here and that they might be here for a few years. She has a sister and a brother who are younger than she is, and she likes basketball, swimming, and computer games."

"She sounds like a lovely girl," said Sophie's mom. "Did you enjoy getting to know her?"

"Uh-huh—she was really nice. There was something different about her, too."

"Really?" said her mom. "What was that?"

"Well, it's just that it seems like so many girls talk mostly about themselves—you know, what they want to do, the clothes they wear, a new hairstyle they want to try, who their friends are, and…I don't know, just lots of stuff. But she wasn't like that. She answered my questions about where they were from and things she liked to do, but then she wanted to know all about me—things about my family and what I enjoyed doing, and she also wanted to know where we went to church. She was just pretty cool…and interesting too! We found out we enjoyed doing many of the same things—and what was really great is that she told me she wonders and has questions about all kinds of things."

Sophie's mom laughed and said, "Well, I can certainly see why that would be special since *someone* around here has many questions about all kinds of things, too."

Sophie joined her mom in laughing and said, "Yes, I guess I do, but I enjoyed being with her, and she made me think about myself."

"In what way?" asked her mom.

"Well, I just thought that it was really special when we had just met, and yet she was interested in who *I* was and what *I* like to do. It made me think she would like for us to be friends, and I think I would enjoy that, too. Maybe that is one of the best ways to have a new friend—you know, to be interested in who *they* are and what *they* like to do. You think so?"

"Yes, I certainly do. Proverbs 18 tells us that to have friends, we must show ourselves to be friendly. I think that was what Rachel did today. She seems like she would be a 'fun' friend. Why don't you get her phone number, and then I will call her mom and see if Rachel would like to come over this weekend."

"Oh, that would be great! I'll talk to her tomorrow. Thanks, Mom."

What Do You Think?

1. Sophie noticed something different about her new friend. What did she notice?
2. Sophie learned one of the best things she could do to have a good friend. What was it?
3. Do you have friends who are like Rachel? Are you a friend like Rachel?

Prayer

Review Memory Verse: "Oil and perfume make the heart glad, and a person's advice is sweet to his friend" (Proverbs 27:9, NASB).

Parent's Guide for Chapter 4 Devotional 2: Sophie's New Friend

Emphasis

To continue illustrating the importance of understanding the characteristics of a good friend.

Scripture Reading: "Whoever heeds life-giving correction will be at home among the wise" (Proverbs 15:31, NIV).

Suggested Answers to "What Do You Think?" Questions

1. What did Aunt Kikky want her friend to tell her when she told her friend about her plans to get married?

    She wanted her friend to agree with her plans and to be excited for her.

2. Was her friend excited? What did her friend tell her?

    No! Aunt Kikky's friend told her she was too young to get married and that she should wait a couple of years and then decide.

3. Did Aunt Kikky like the advice from her friend? What did she decide to do? What happened when she went off to college?

    No! After Aunt Kikky thought about her friend's advice, she decided her friend was right, and she went on to college, where she met Uncle Mike—and then she realized she would have made a big mistake if she had agreed to get married and not gone to college.

4. A few years later, Aunt Kikky read about the good counsel of a friend. Who did that make her think of?

   Her very good friend who told her the truth—not just what she wanted to hear

Prayer

That we all can be as wise as her friend.

Review Memory Verse: "Oil and perfume make the heart glad, and a person's advice is sweet to his friend" (Proverbs 27:9, NASB).

Chapter 4 Devotional 3: Listening to Good Advice

Scripture Reading: "Whoever heeds life-giving correction will be at home among the wise" (Proverbs 15:31, NIV).

"Sophie, did I tell you I called Mrs. Palmer about Rachel coming over on Saturday?" said her mom as she was preparing dinner.

Sophie looked up from the homework she was doing at the breakfast bar and replied excitedly, "No, you didn't. What did she say?"

"I called her on the way to work this morning. We visited on the phone for a while and talked about her move and all the details that go with that. She said Rachel had told her she had talked with you at school and hoped you both could be friends. So I invited Rachel to come over on Saturday afternoon. Her mom is going to bring her so we can meet also. We'll have a cup of coffee and get acquainted, and then later, I'll take Rachel home. Does that sound okay?"

"That sounds great! Tomorrow I'll see Rachel at school, and we'll make plans. I think she and I are going to be good friends. After school today, I went over and saw Aunt Kikky, and we talked about having good friends."

"You did? I'm sure that was fun; Aunt Kikky knows a lot about establishing good friends. What did she have to say?"

"Well," Sophie replied, "she was asking about our study in Proverbs and what we were reading about. I told her we had been talking about our friends and how important they can be to us. She agreed, and then she told me the same verse that we have been memorizing—you know, 'The heartfelt counsel of a friend is as sweet as perfume and incense' [Proverbs 27:9, NLT]. I laughed and told her that was our memory verse for the week."

Sophie's mom smiled and said, "That was a little unusual, wasn't it—that she would give you the same verse we have been working on?"

"Yes, she said that too—but then she told me why that verse meant so much to her."

"And why was that?" asked her mom.

"Aunt Kikky told me of a time when she was trying to make a decision about going away to school or getting married. She really was just thinking about it—she hadn't even said anything to her parents yet, but her friend knew she was getting serious about her boyfriend, and she asked her what she was going to do. So Aunt Kikky told her what she was thinking about. She said she wanted her friend to get excited about a wedding and tell her that she could get married and go to school at the local community college—so she could have the best of both worlds."

"But she didn't do that?" her mom interjected.

"Nope!" said Sophie. "Her friend told her she thought Aunt Kikky was too young to get married and that she should go on to college as she had planned. If her love for her boyfriend was the real thing, it would still be there in a couple of years, and she could rethink it then. Aunt Kikky said she didn't like that advice…but the more she thought about it, the more she realized her friend was right. Then I jumped into the story and said, 'So, you went off to college and married Uncle Mike when you got back?' And then Aunt Kikky said, 'Goodness no!' She told me she met Uncle Mike at college and that it didn't take her long to realize she would have made a huge mistake if she had stayed at home and gone to the community college. Then one day, a few years later, as she was reading in Proverbs about *the heartfelt counsel of a friend being as sweet as perfume*, Aunt Kikky realized how much her friend had really helped her. Mom, she said to me, 'Sophie, my friend told me the *truth* rather than just joining in with me in something that would have been exciting…but would have had terrible results!' That's really something, isn't it?"

"Yes, that *is* amazing!" her mom replied. "I didn't know your Aunt Kikky then and had never heard that story."

"Well," said Sophie, "it just makes me wonder."

Sophie's mom laughed and said, "And what do you wonder about this time?"

"I just wonder if I could be that wise," replied Sophie.

Her mom came around the bar and gave Sophie a hug. "You know, I think you will be that wise when some of those important decisions come along. You know why?"

"No," said Sophie. "Why?"

"Well…you are now ten years old, and you *want* to be wise—and I believe your heart will grow stronger in its purpose and desire to be wise. It's good to wonder, but you don't have to worry; remember, it is the Lord who is '*all wisdom*,' and He will continue to help you—just like I think He is helping you now by giving you a new good friend. So, let's talk about what you girls can do on Saturday."

What Do You Think?

1. What did Aunt Kikky want her friend to tell her when she told her friend about her plans to get married? Was her friend excited? What did her friend tell her?
2. Did Aunt Kikky like the advice from her friend? What did she decide to do? What happened when she went to college?
3. A few years later, Aunt Kikky read about the good counsel of a friend. Who did that make her think of?

Prayer

That we all can be as wise as her friend.

Review Memory Verse: "Oil and perfume make the heart glad, and a person's advice is sweet to his friend" (Proverbs 27:9, NASB).

CHAPTER 5:
The Deep and Terrible Woods

Parent's Guide for Chapter 5: The *Deep* and *Terrible* Woods— Disobedience

Emphasis

Sophie, Mary Sue (Sophie's friend), and Jackson spend the afternoon with another friend (Andy), who influences them to go into a forbidden part of the woods. This chapter presents a situation that many children face when they need to say "no" to an activity but do not know how to do it without feeling embarrassed.

Memory Verse:

"Ponder the path of your feet; then all your ways will be sure" (Proverbs 4:26, ESV).

Suggested Answers to "What Do You Think?" Questions

1. What do you think it means to "Give careful thought to the paths for your feet"?

    "Careful thought" = to think about carefully, especially before making a decision or reaching a conclusion; to consider, to review, to meditate on.

2. What could you do to help you remember to "give careful thought"?

    Keep a diary, pray every day, asking God to help you think as He thinks.

3. What is the promise of this verse?

   If you take time to think about what you're going to do before you actually do it, you will make better decisions.

Prayer

Review Memory Verse: "Ponder the path of your feet; then all your ways will be sure" (Proverbs 4:26, ESV).

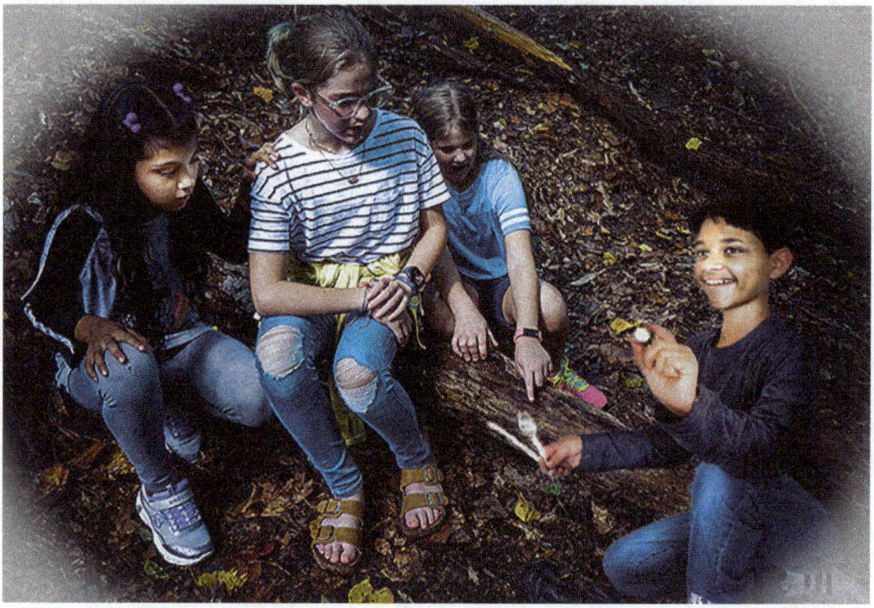

Chapter Five:
The *Deep* and *Terrible* Woods—
Disobedience

Sophie, Jackson, Mary Sue, and Andy were having a great time riding their bikes on the bike trails surrounding their neighborhood. Mary Sue had come over to play with Sophie after school, and Andy had come to play with Jackson. Since they were all riding bicycles, they decided to go together and were soon racing each other from one landmark to another. This was easy to do because there was the huge sycamore tree that the bike trail circled, the old Civil War landmark that the trail passed by, the entrance to the park in which they all played, and other places that were easy to remember. It was a terrific bike trail because the trails were paved and wide enough so that two bicyclers could easily ride side by side, and the kids were having a great time. They stopped by the water fountain to rest for a while; after a few minutes, Andy said, "Where does that side trail go?"

Jackson replied, his voice sounding like the voices in a ghost story, "That goes to the *deep and terrible woods!*"

They all laughed, and Sophie explained, "It's really swampy back there with big mud holes; and after a little bit, the trail becomes a path, and then it stops altogether—so we aren't allowed to go back there."

Mimicking Jackson's ghostly voice, Andy asked, "*Is it haunted?*"

"No, of course not!" Jackson replied.

"You know how parents can be," said Sophie in her grown-up voice. "They usually exaggerate those kinds of things, so we won't even think about doing them." As soon as she said that, she thought, *I didn't mean for that to sound quite like it came out,* but she didn't know how to correct it without being embarrassed—so she said nothing.

"You're right, Sophie," said Andy, "and I think it would be really fun to explore back there."

"I do, too," said Jackson, "but I'm not sure it's safe."

Mary Sue quickly said, "I'm not either."

"Oh, come on," said Andy. "It's within the city limits—how could it be so bad? Besides, we don't have to go very far; we could just go a little way, and if it begins to look [his voice changing to the ghostly sound] *deeeep and terrible*, we can just turn around and come back."

"Well, I guess that's true," said Jackson.

"Maybe," said Mary Sue.

Sophie was getting more uncomfortable by the minute, but she didn't know how to get out of this. So she spoke up and said, "I don't know, guys—I'm sure our parents just want us to be safe."

"Well, of course, they do," said Andy, "but as you said, they 'always exaggerate' these things. What if we just go down the trail for a little way, and if it looks bad, we can decide right away that they were right, and we will turn around and come back? It could be a great adventure."

Sophie's heart sank, but she knew they would all think she was a scaredy cat if she didn't go along, so she said, "Okay, we can go just a little way. Is that all right with you, Mary Sue?"

"I guess so," she answered. "What do you think, Jackson?"

Jackson was uncomfortable also, but he was too embarrassed to say anything, so he chimed in right along with Andy. "We'll just go a little way."

So, reluctantly, walking their bikes, Sophie, Jackson, and Mary Sue followed Andy down the trail that led into the woods. At first, they all walked slowly and said very little; but as they continued, it did indeed seem more and more like a great adventure, so that soon you could hear excited voices, "Hey, look at this tree—you can see where the lightning struck it big time!" and "Look, guys—they must have been racing motorbikes back here; the tracks are everywhere."

They soon decided to park their bicycles so they could explore better. A few minutes passed when they came to an old shack that was overgrown with bushes and weeds. Sophie and Mary Sue were frightened when they first saw it; Andy and Jackson were frightened also…they just wouldn't admit it. But when they realized the shack was really old and that the windows were all broken and smashed in and that the door was ajar, they forgot their fear and went to investigate. Andy was the first to get there; when he tried to open the door, it fell off its hinges and came crashing down. They all jumped back—but soon overcame their nervousness and investigated more thoroughly. As they peeked inside, they saw some old newspapers and empty tin cans. Over in the corner, something was covered up with a tattered, dirty blanket. This time Jackson ventured forth and carefully pulled the blanket away. He yelled, "Oh, no!" Sophie, Mary Sue, and Andy all screamed at the same time, "What is it?" Then Jackson turned around and said, "*Gotcha!*" and doubled over with laughter. "That's *not* funny, Jackson," said Mary Sue and Sophie—but Andy just laughed. Hidden under the blanket were more tin cans and old newspapers, so they all turned around and left and continued down the trail. As each one would find something of interest, he or she would call to the others to come and see. Jackson found a stack of rocks and yelled for them to come over; when they all got there, he removed the rocks. Underneath were three feathers, a spoon, an old movie pass, three nickels, and a quarter. He started to share the change with them but then changed his mind saying, "No…I don't know who left it here, but they may come back to get it; I'm just going to put it back." So they helped him put everything back the way it was, and then they moved on.

As they continued on, they often had to go around a mud puddle; and as the trail narrowed, it also began to be overgrown with parts of dead trees and bushes and tall weeds. Soon the trail became just a small pathway, and mud puddles were everywhere. As they made their way around all of the obstacles, Sophie realized that it was beginning to get dark. Then she looked over at Mary Sue and saw that her new tennis shoes were really dirty, which made her look at hers, and she realized what a mess she was. As they were going around a big pile of leaves—and before they realized it—they all had stepped into soft ground, which was the beginning of a huge mud puddle. It seemed more like a mud and water pond because their feet sunk almost up to their ankles. Just about that time, Mary Sue screamed, "Look!" And before their eyes was a great big snake crawling out of the other side of the pond and into the bushes. Suddenly, without any hesitation, each one came out of the mud and ran, as fast as their legs would carry them, back to where the trail was wider and where they had left their bikes. By this time, Sophie was nearly in tears, though she managed to hide her feelings from everyone. She knew her mom was going to be so upset and that she was in trouble! But that wasn't the only thing that bothered her. She was angry with herself because she had let herself get into this mess. She knew she should never have agreed with this so-called adventure and that she should have been strong enough to say *no*! But she also knew it might never have started if she had not made that ridiculous *crack* about parents' exaggerations about what could happen to them and that her mom's instruction about the trail was for her own safety. So even though she wasn't really sure about the best way to say it, she turned to the others and said, "Okay, we should have never done this, and I'm sorry that I didn't say so from the beginning! We need to go home."

So quietly and sheepishly, they all got back on their bikes and went home to face the *deep and terrible* trouble.

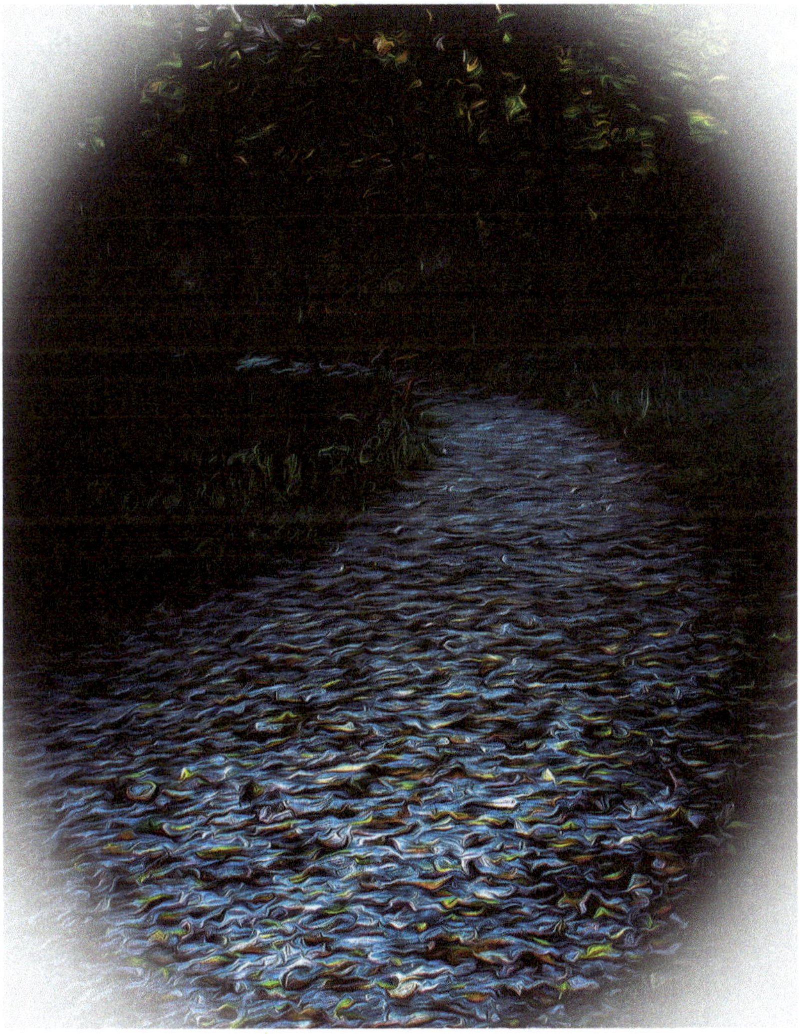

What Do You Think?

1. What do you think it means to "ponder the path of your feet"?
2. What could you do to help you remember to "ponder the path of your feet"?
3. What is the promise of this verse?

Prayer

Review Memory Verse: "Ponder the path of your feet; then all your ways will be sure" (Proverbs 4:26, ESV).

SUPPLY LIST FOR ACTIVITY 5

Make copies of the roleplays at the end of the chapter.

* * *

Activity 5

The following three roleplaying scenes contain mock conversations to help your children avoid getting into situations like Sophie and Jackson did. Roleplaying is an excellent way to give young people a tool to use. Situations in life can begin very innocently but quickly become a means to deter children from what they know is the truth. When children get into a situation they do not know how to handle, these conversations stored in their memories can be just the tool they need to stand firm! Be creative—a child can first play the antagonist, and the next time, play the one who is avoiding the temptation.

- Roleplay #1: Skateboarding
- Roleplay #2: Looking Stylish
- Roleplay #3: "But Everyone Does It!"

Supplies

Make copies of the roleplays for each character.

Roleplay 1: Skateboarding

Characters: Randy, Jake

Randy: "Hi Jake, what's up?"

Jake: "Nothing much. I'm just going over to the park to do some rounds on my skateboard."

Randy: "Do you mind if I come along?"

Jake: "Course not—come on, we'll take turns doing spins."

Randy: "Okay, but you know what? It's a lot more fun behind the old grocery store. There are some good trails there that are beaten down, and a lot of guys go over there."

Jake: "Yeah, I heard it was fun—but I also heard there are some older kids who hang out a lot over there and sometimes get into trouble with the police."

Randy: "Well, that might be true, but there are also boys our age that go just to ride skateboards—and those older guys don't bother us; in fact, some of them are pretty cool and even talk to us sometimes."

Jake: "Really?"

Randy: "Sure do, so let's try it out!"

Jake: "I don't know…I don't think my dad would like it."

Randy: "Your dad! He doesn't even have to know."

Jake: "Well [he pauses and thinks a minute], that may be true—*but I would know*—and I just think I'd rather go to the park. Besides, I'd like to go to the ice cream shop afterward for a glass of water and an ice cream cone."

Randy: "Ice cream?"

Jake: "Yeah…I probably have enough money for two."

Randy: "Oh…well, maybe I'll come along with you—but Jake?"

Jake: "Yeah?"

Randy: "You're kind of weird!"

Jake: "Maybe."

What do you think?

Roleplay 2: Looking Stylish

Characters: Sarah, Tracy, Susan, and Tori (eleven-year-old girls in the sixth grade)

Sarah, Tracy, Susan, and Tori are in the restroom at school after gym class, changing from their gym clothes into their regular clothes. Sarah, Tracy, and Susan are brushing their hair in front of the mirrors while Tori is still changing her clothes over by the lockers.

Sarah: "Did you see Betsy's outfit this morning? She looked like she was in a fright show and forgot to change costumes!"

Tracy: [laughing] "Isn't that the truth! Seems like her mom would tell her how to put her clothes together, doesn't it?"

Susan: [laughing] "I almost laughed out loud when she came in. And I heard you snickering, Sarah."

Sarah: "Well, I just couldn't help it. It was really awful."

Tracy: "I know we are supposed to be friendly to new kids, but it's kind of embarrassing to be seen with her."

Tori walks up to brush her hair and enters the conversation.

Tori: "Have you girls met her?"

Sarah: "No! Why would I want to?"

Tori: "Because if you did, you might find out that her mom died last year and that she lives with her dad and two older brothers—and I'm sure they don't know the latest styles for ten and eleven-year-old girls!"

Sarah: "Oh…we didn't know that."

Susan: "No, we didn't…that's really tough about losing her mom."

Tracy: "I guess we kind of jumped to conclusions, didn't we?"

Tori: "I just think that when we take the time to know someone, it's easier to understand when they don't seem to fit in."

Susan: "You're right, Tori—I was pretty rude, and I'm sorry. Do you have any suggestions?"

Sarah and Tracy: "Yeah—is there something we can do?"

Tori: "Well…I heard Mrs. Morgan say she was going to have an extra class after school for the girls who were interested in learning about how to coordinate clothes and colors. If we went and asked Betsy to come along, perhaps we could all learn something. In the meantime, if we just try to include her at lunch or at P.E., maybe she would feel a lot better about school."

Roleplay 3: "But Everyone Does It!"

Characters: Saleslady, Emily, Allyson, Jenna

Emily, Allyson, and Jenna are at the mall picking up a package, and afterward, they are all going to the theater.

Saleslady: "That will be $3.50, please."

Emily: "Okay." [hands her a $5.00 bill]

Saleslady: [hands Emily her package and change] "Here's your change; thank you—and you girls have a great day!"

Allyson: "She was a nice saleslady, wasn't she?"

Emily: "She sure was—she gave me a dollar extra in change!"

Allyson: "You're kidding!"

Emily: "Nope—here it is [shows it to the girls]—an extra dollar!"

Jenna: "You aren't going to keep it, are you?"

Emily: "I don't know why not—it was *her* mistake! Besides, we can stop at the Dollar Store, and I'll get us a bag of candy for the movie."

Allyson: "Yeah—that would be great!"

Jenna: "But it isn't your dollar!"

Allyson: "Oh Jenna, don't be such a goody-goody—it's just a dollar!"

Emily: "Yeah, Jenna; sometimes you can be such a killjoy!"

Jenna: "Perhaps I am—and I don't want to ruin your good time…but it's the same as stealing, Emily, and that saleslady will have to make it up when her cash register doesn't balance tonight."

Emily: "How do you know that? Besides, it's just a dollar—everyone does this kind of thing."

Jenna: "Not everyone, Emily. And my sister uses a cash register at work, and that's how I know. I think there are lots of people who would give it back—and that's exactly what you should do!"

Emily: "Well, I don't think they do, and I'm not taking it back! And if you don't like it, you can just go home, and Allyson and I will go to the movie!"

Jenna: "I'm sorry, Emily. I didn't want to cause trouble, but I think it's wrong. I'll call my mom and ask her to come to pick me up."

Emily: "Okay—see you later, Miss Goody-Goody!"

Parent's Guide for Chapter 5 Devotional 1: Elizabeth's Story

Emphasis

Elizabeth relates one of her failures to Sophie and explains how she was comforted by their mother.

Scripture Reading: "For as high as the heavens are above the earth, so great is His love for those who fear Him; as far as the east is from the west, so far has He removed our transgressions from us" (Psalm 103:11–12, NIV).

Suggested Answers to "What Do You Think?" Questions

1. What can we be sure of whenever we fail or sin?

    God loves us. When we ask Him to forgive us, He always does!

2. Look at a globe or map of the earth. What do you think "as far as the east is from the west" means?

    If you keep going east, you will never hit west!

3. When someone asks you to do something that you know is wrong, why is it so hard to say "no"?

    Fear of rejection, fear of being laughed at, fear of losing a friend, fear of not having any friends…

4. Do you have any friends who are easily persuaded to disobey or who do not seem to care when they disobey? How could you help them?

   Be obedient in your own life and set a good example.

Prayer

Review Memory Verse: "Ponder the paths of your feet; then all your ways will be sure" (Proverbs 4:26, ESV).

Chapter 5 Devotional 1: Elizabeth's Story

Scripture Reading: "For as high as the heavens are above the earth, so great is His love for those who fear him; as far as the east is from the west, so far has He removed our transgressions from us" (Psalm 103:11–12, NIV).

Sophie was in her room getting ready for bed. She had put on her pajamas and was brushing her teeth when Elizabeth knocked at the door and said, "Hey, Sophie, can I come in?"

"Sure," replied Sophie. "I would love some company."

"It was a tough day, wasn't it?" said Elizabeth.

"Well, it started out okay…but then I really blew it!"

"I know—Mom was really upset—but mostly, she was afraid that something had happened to you. I was late coming home too, so I couldn't go looking for you."

"Yeah," said Sophie, "but you called her and told her you would be late because of practice. Why can't I think of the right thing to do when I should?"

"Don't be so hard on yourself, Sophie; remember, I'm five years older than you. And I certainly don't always do it right! Did I ever tell you about the time I let a girl talk me into giving her answers to a test?"

"No!" said Sophie. "That's like cheating, isn't it? Why did you do that?"

"Probably for the same reason you and Jackson let Andy talk you into going into those woods. It happened when I was in the fifth grade. This girl was very popular, and everyone thought she was funny and smart—and all the boys liked her. The class had already taken the test, but she came in right before lunchtime with an excuse note from her mom. When we went to lunch, she came right over to my table, sat down, and began talking to me like we were best friends. She had hardly said anything to me before then. She began talking about our getting together, how she wanted us to be good friends, and how she wanted to know my opinions about many of the things she was doing. Then she started telling me about being so sick the night before that she just couldn't study and that now she was afraid she was going to fail the test—*plus*, the teacher had told her she would have to take it right after lunch. She was something of an expert at twisting things, Sophie! Before I knew it, I was telling her everything I could remember that was on that test—including the answers. When the bell rang to go back to class, and the teacher gave her the test, she looked at me and winked…and my heart sank! It seemed like it all happened so fast. First, the class took the test, then she came in late, and then we went to lunch, where we talked the entire time, and then we were back in class, and she was taking the test. After class, she wouldn't even look at me, and she's hardly spoken to me since that day."

"Oh, Elizabeth, that's awful!" said Sophie.

"What was really awful was that I realized how easily I had been swayed to do something I knew was wrong. When I came home, Mom knew something was wrong, and I finally told her what I had done."

"Was she really mad?" asked Sophie.

"No, she wasn't angry…but she was sad. I told her I was sorry because I knew I had really disappointed her, and I felt so guilty about all of it. I had asked Jesus to forgive me…but I still felt guilty. I won't ever forget what she said!"

"What was that?" interrupted Sophie.

"She put her arms around me and said, 'Elizabeth, just remember that when we confess our sins, God removes them from us as far as the east is from the west. That is promised to us in Psalm 103. The guilt of our sin can never return…any more than the east can become west or the west can become east! Jesus forever stands between us and our sin!' It was a good thing to learn," continued Elizabeth, "and I have never forgotten it!"

"Thanks, Elizabeth," said Sophie. "I'm glad you told me. Sometimes I think I'm the only one who messes up around here."

Elizabeth laughed and said, "No, silly, there's plenty of 'messing up' to go around! And I had my consequences to pay, too. It wasn't easy going back to the teacher and telling her what I did. I got an F on that test and had to do a lot of extra studies to make up for it. But I didn't mind—I was just happy to know it was taken care of. And now I'm going to take care of getting myself ready for bed. Goodnight, Sophie—see you in the morning."

"Goodnight, Elizabeth; thanks for telling me your story."

What Do You Think?

1. What can we be sure of whenever we fail or sin?
2. Look at a globe or map of the earth. What do you think "as far as the east is from the west" means?
3. When someone asks you to do something that you know is wrong, why is it so hard to say "no"?
4. Do you have any friends who are easily persuaded to disobey or who do not seem to care when they disobey? How could you help them?

Prayer

Review Memory Verse: "Ponder the path of your feet; then all your ways will be sure" (Proverbs 4:26, ESV).

Parent's Guide for Chapter 5 Devotional 2: Let the Children Come to Me

Emphasis

Sophie wants to know if Jesus "gets mad at us when we sin." This devotional is designed to assure children that Jesus forgives, that He understands us better than we understand ourselves, and that He places great importance on children—as shown in the New Testament by His interaction with them.

Scripture Reading: "See that you do not despise one of these little ones. For I tell you that their angels in heaven always see the face of my Father in heaven" (Matthew 18:10, NIV).

Suggested Answers to "What Do You Think?" Questions

1. If Jesus were at the seashore and saw you playing in the sand, what do you think He might do? What do you think Jesus does when you are at home doing homework? Or at night when you go to sleep? Or when you are afraid? Or when you do something you know is wrong?

    He comes to play with me, helps me think, stays with me, tells me He is with me and not to be afraid, and tells me He still loves me.

2. Is there another verse you have memorized or read that tells you how Jesus responds to you?

   He always gives assurance of His great love for children as in the following verse, "Let the little children come to Me, and do not hinder them, for the kingdom of heaven belongs to such as these" (Matthew 19:14, NIV).

   "Every word of God is flawless; He is a shield to those who take refuge in Him" (Proverbs 30:5, NIV). From Chapter 1, Devotional 3.

Prayer

Review Memory Verse: "Ponder the path of your feet; then all your ways will be sure" (Proverbs 4:26, ESV).

Chapter 5 Devotional 2: Let the Children Come to Me

Scripture Reading: "See that you do not look down on one of these little ones. For I tell you that their angels in heaven always see the face of my Father in heaven" (Matthew 18:10, NIV).

Sophie's mom came into Sophie's room to pray with her before she went to sleep. She sat down next to Sophie on her bed, and immediately, Sophie said, "Mom?"

"Yes," replied her mother.

"Do you think Jesus gets mad at us when we sin?"

"Why would you think that, Sophie?"

"I'm not sure…maybe just because I feel so guilty when I do something wrong. I can understand if Mary Sue's mom is mad at me for taking Mary Sue into those woods."

"Did you think she was angry with you when you told her what happened? I think I heard you tell her that you were very sorry."

"Yes, I did, and I don't think she was angry—but I think she was disappointed."

"Well, I'm sure she was. That is part of the consequences we bear when we do something wrong. But she also understands that kids forget and can get themselves into all kinds of situations."

"Uh-huh, she was really kind about it."

"So…if she can understand, don't you think Jesus understands too?"

"I know," said Sophie, "but sometimes I wish we could just see Him and hear Him say He understands."

"Yes," replied her mom. "Many of us have felt that way sometimes. But remember, we have many reasons why we can believe He hears, understands, and forgives."

"Like the one you told Elizabeth when she helped someone cheat on a test?"

"She told you about that?"

"Yes...she did...the one about our sins being separated from us as far as the east is from the west. That means they can never meet up with us again, doesn't it, Mom?"

"It certainly does," continued her mom. "Do you remember when the disciples wouldn't let the little children come to Jesus for a blessing?"

"Oh yes, that's right!" interrupted Sophie. "He told them to let the little children come to Him for...for...what was the rest of it?"

"Let me see if I can find it quickly," said her mom. She picked up Sophie's Bible. "I think it's in Matthew." She turned to the Book of Matthew and began to flip through it. "Here it is—it's in Matthew 19... verse 14!" Reading out loud, she began, "Let the little children come to me, and do not hinder them, for the kingdom of heaven belongs to such as these."

"So that's for me, isn't it, Mom?"

"Absolutely! He knows you are a young girl who is going to sin and make mistakes, but He also knows your heart—which is so dear to Him."

"You know what, Mom?"

"What?" said her mom.

"I just have so many things to wonder about...I don't know if I can get around to all of them." Sophie's mom laughed, gave her a hug, and said, "Okay, hon, why don't we just say a goodnight prayer, and you can wonder as much as you like before you go to sleep."

"Okay, Mom—it's just that sometimes I wonder why I wonder so much!"

What Do You Think?

1. If Jesus were at the seashore and saw you playing in the sand, what do you think He might do? What do you think Jesus does when you are at home doing homework? Or at night when you go to sleep? Or when you are afraid? Or when you do something you know is wrong?
2. Is there another verse you have memorized or read that tells you how Jesus responds to you?

Prayer

Review Memory Verse: "Ponder the path of your feet; then all your ways will be sure" (Proverbs 4:26, ESV).

Parent's Guide for Chapter 5 Devotional 3: Samson and Delilah

Emphasis

The story about Samson shows children that adults make really serious mistakes in their lives—and that sometimes the consequences of those mistakes are severe! However, when our Heavenly Father hears our earnest prayers admitting our mistakes and asking for forgiveness, He really does remember our sins <u>no more</u> and counts us among the faithful.

Scripture Reading: "My son, do not let wisdom and understanding out of your sight, preserve sound judgment and discretion; they will be life for you, an ornament to grace your neck. Then you will go on your way in safety, and your foot will not stumble" (Proverbs 3:21–23, NIV).

Suggested Answers to "What Do You Think?" Questions

1. Do your parents ever make mistakes? *[smile, parents]* When they apologize, how does it make you feel?

   Everyone makes mistakes, even parents!

2. How do you feel about Samson and Delilah? Is Samson's story scary? Is it hard to believe how wicked Delilah was?

3. What is the most encouraging part of the story of Samson and Delilah?

The end, when Samson relies on God to help him do the right thing

4. What is the Hall of Faith that is mentioned in this story?

   Hebrews 11:11

Prayer

Review Memory Verse: "Ponder the path of your feet; then all your ways will be sure" (Proverbs 4:26, ESV).

Chapter 5 Devotional 3: Samson and Delilah

Scripture Reading: "My son, do not let wisdom and understanding out of your sight, preserve sound judgment and discretion; they will be life for you, an ornament to grace your neck. Then you will go on your way in safety, and your foot will not stumble" (Proverbs 3:21–23, NIV).

"Our Sunday school lesson today was about Samson and Delilah, Mom," said Sophie. She, her mom, and Elizabeth had left church and were on their way to get lunch.

"It was? Well, how was it?" asked her mom.

"Really good…all about making the right choices…You didn't call Mrs. Hanson and tell her about us going into the woods, did you?"

Sophie's mom laughed and said, "No, of course not! I'm sure those lessons were planned several months ago—and I wouldn't do anything like that. Besides, the lessons we learn from Samson are things we all need to be reminded of occasionally."

"Well," Sophie said, "for a grown man and also a judge of Israel, he wasn't very wise! It seems like he would have caught on after Delilah kept on asking and asking where he got his strength."

"You're right, Sophie," Elizabeth spoke up, "he was gullible and…"

"Gullible?" interrupted Sophie. "What does that mean?"

"It means," Elizabeth continued, "that he was easily deceived because he wanted her to love him and that he was taken in by her beauty and her lies."

"That was dumb!" said Sophie.

"Help me out, Mom," said Elizabeth.

Sophie's mom grinned and said, "Okay…Yes, Sophie, I guess you could say that. I'm sure Mrs. Hanson told you that Samson had been chosen by God for a special purpose and had taken the Nazirite vow; part of that vow was that his hair would never be cut. As he grew up and became stronger and stronger, he had many victories over the Philistines—and his fame became known throughout the region. Sometimes when people become famous, they also become more easily influenced or tempted to do wrong…and they begin to think that they cannot fail."

"But Mom," Sophie interrupted, "it seems Samson forgot all about what God had called him to do!"

"That's true, but do you remember the verse from Proverbs about guarding your heart?"

"Yes, but I don't think I can say it all…something about guarding your heart because everything comes from it."

"That's really good! I think it goes, 'Above all else, guard your heart, for everything you do flows from it.' When Samson wanted the love of Delilah more than anything else, his heart led him right into the enemy's territory. She was constantly leading him into situations where he would eventually give in and tell her what she wanted to hear. Did Mrs. Hanson finish the story for you?"

"Oh yes!" replied Sophie. "She told us how Samson finally gave in and told Delilah that his strength came from his hair that had never been cut. Delilah told the Philistines, who came in while Samson was sleeping and cut off his hair. Samson's strength then left him, and the Philistines made him a slave grinding grain in the dungeons. Then they took him to a big feast to show off the prisoner they had caught, but in all of their excitement, they didn't think about his hair growing back. So when Samson arrived at the feast, he prayed to God to help him destroy the temple where they were all eating. The Philistines had chained him between two columns, and because Samson's strength had returned, he pulled on the chains, the columns broke, and the whole temple came down—killing everyone…including himself! It's a really sad story…and kind of scary. But Mrs. Hanson made me feel a lot better about it."

"What did she say?" asked her mom.

"She said the New Testament doesn't list all of his failures; it lists Samson in the *Hall of Faith*—you know, where it talks about all the heroes in the Bible—and that when we turn to God, He will still use us…no matter how imperfect we are!"

"She's right. I'm sure when Samson was in that prison that he had many regrets and was deeply sorry and asked for forgiveness for his sin. He realized he had failed! He had also been humbled—and that was when he prayed to God."

"I felt like that too when I let Andy convince me that it was okay to go into the woods," replied Sophie.

"Oh, Sophie, I know you disobeyed and had to deal with the consequences, but you are a long way from being a Samson! We all fail, even when we are trying to *guard* our hearts, because we are still very human. The great joy is that when we are forgiven, we start fresh and can live our lives with greater wisdom because we have learned from our mistakes."

"Thank you, uh…do you think we could stop for lunch now? I'm really hungry!"

"Yes," Elizabeth said, "our favorite pizza place is just ahead on the right."

"Okay, girls; great suggestion, Elizabeth—I'm hungry too!"

What Do You Think?

1. Do your parents ever make mistakes? When they apologize, how does it make you feel?
2. How do you feel about Samson and Delilah? Is Samson's story scary? Is it hard to believe how wicked Delilah was?
3. What is the most encouraging part of the story of Samson and Delilah?
4. What is the *Hall of Faith* that is mentioned in this story?

Prayer

Review Memory Verse: "Ponder the path of your feet; then all your ways will be sure" (Proverbs 4:26, ESV).

CHAPTER 6: The *Deep* and *Terrible* Trouble

Parent's Guide for Chapter 6: The *Deep* and *Terrible* Trouble—Consequences

Emphasis

Sophie and Jackson go home to face the consequences of their actions. Sophie sees the sorrow and fear her mom had when she thought they might be hurt. Sophie learns that while consequences are not any fun, "the part I hate the most is when I felt so guilty because I knew that what I was thinking of doing was wrong—<u>and I did it anyway!</u>"

Memory Verse: "My son, do not forget my teaching, but keep my commands in your heart, for they will prolong your life many years and bring you peace and prosperity" (Proverbs 3:1–2, NIV).

Suggested Answers to "What Do You Think?" Questions

1. Sophie disobeyed her mother and had to apologize to Mary Sue's mom, clean her room really well, and do the dishes for a week. Do you think Sophie's consequences were too hard, too easy, or appropriate?

    Your child's answer will depend on age and your expectations.

2. Can you think of any consequences that might have been better?

    You might also ask your child what his/her consequences for disobedience should be.

3. What is the most difficult thing about getting into trouble?

   Fear of what the consequences will be, fear of what other people will think of you, feeling guilty, disappointing your parents

4. What was the hardest thing for Sophie?

   Feeling guilty

Prayer

Review Memory Verse: "My son, do not forget my teaching, but keep my commands in your heart, for they will prolong your life many years and bring you peace and prosperity" (Proverbs 3:1–2, NIV).

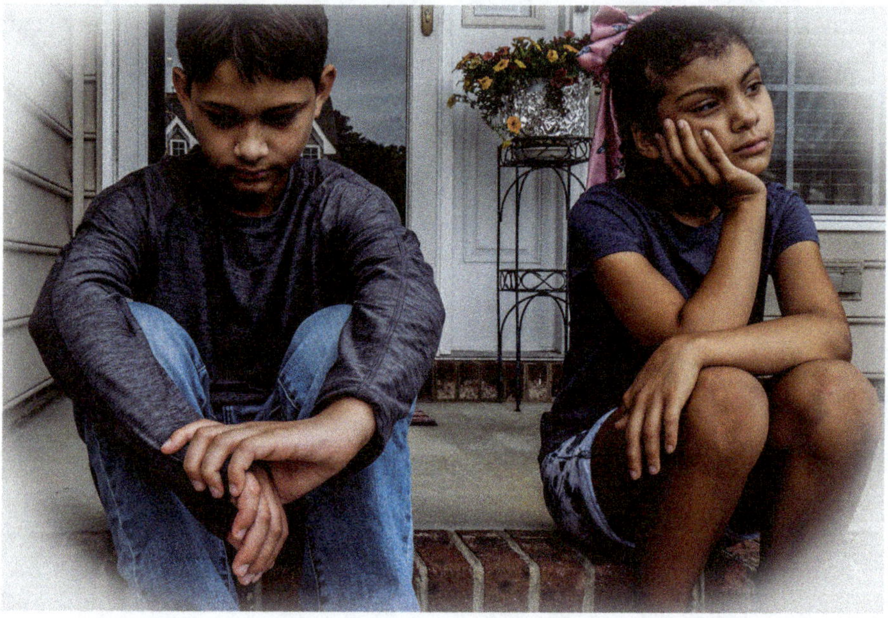

Chapter Six:
The *Deep* and *Terrible* Trouble—Consequences

Sophie sat on the porch in front of her house and watched next door as Jackson pulled up weeds from the flower beds. She could tell he had been busy for a while because his trash bag looked like it was almost full. In a few minutes, he stood up and put a twist tie around the top of the bag, walked to the side of the house, and dropped the bag into the garbage can. Then he looked up and saw Sophie. He waved, walked over, and sat down beside her.

"Hi, Jackson," Sophie said.

"Hi, Sophie…you all right today?" Jackson replied.

"You mean after that bummer of a day yesterday?" Sophie responded.

"Yeah…it really *was* bad, wasn't it? What happened when you got home?"

"Well—when Mary Sue and I came in, Mom looked frightened and asked us if we were all right. I told her that we were fine and that we just didn't realize what time it was. When we admitted to getting kind of muddy, she wanted to know exactly *how* we got so muddy. I wanted to tell her the whole story—she was going to find out anyway—and to tell the truth, I just wanted to get it all out so I could feel better…but I was so upset that I didn't explain it very well. I did say enough for her to know I had disobeyed her and caused Mary Sue to just about ruin her shoes and get mud all over her clothes."

"Then what happened?" asked Jackson.

Sophie continued, "It just got worse! Mom was really quiet at first, and then she told us to go into the bathroom and try to get ourselves cleaned up as best as we could. She said she was going to call Mary Sue's mom and tell her she could come by and pick up Mary Sue. Mom also said that she fully expected me to apologize for Mary Sue's clothes and shoes being such a mess and then explain to her what happened and tell her that it would not happen again. By the time Mary Sue and I washed off as much mud as we could, her mother rang the doorbell. I was really scared of what her mother would say—and I know I didn't do it well, but I told her I was so sorry and tried to explain what happened. Then I promised her we would never go down that path again. You could tell she was disappointed, but I guess she was sort of polite about it. She told me that we all make mistakes and that she was sure this particular one wouldn't happen again. Then they said goodbye and left."

Jackson had been looking out in the street, but when Sophie finished telling him what had happened, he looked at her and said, "So the worst is yet to come, isn't it?"

Sophie sighed and said, "It certainly is! When I turned around, Mom was walking into the living room. I followed her, and when I walked into the room, she was sitting in the chair with her back to me. I stood there for a minute…she was so quiet. I thought, *Oh my, she is really mad—I better get this over with*, and I walked around her chair and sat down across from her. I just knew she was really angry…but when I looked up at her, tears were running down her face. She was crying, Jackson…*she was crying*! My mom gets tears in her eyes every so often—usually when she's praying for us and sometimes when she tells us how much she loves us—but she doesn't cry when we do things wrong! I didn't know what to do! I had already told her I was really sorry and that I wouldn't do it again. I tried to think of something else to say, but I just couldn't…so I just sat there."

Sophie paused and then went on, "It seemed like it was forever, but it was probably just a few minutes when Mom wiped her eyes and blew her nose…and then she looked at me and said she was so sorry that she broke down and cried. She told me that it had been a rough day at the office, and she had been late leaving. When she got into her car, she noticed that she was very low on gas—she barely made it to the gas station! Then Elizabeth called her to say that she was running late—so then Mom was worried about me being at home by myself. When she got home, and I wasn't there, she was really worried. Then—to top it all off—she went into the kitchen and realized the dishes in the dishwasher had not been washed. She turned the dishwasher on, and nothing happened—it wasn't working! Then I came in, and at first, she was afraid something bad had happened to me. When I told her what had happened, she was so relieved that we weren't hurt—but then was so disappointed that I had disobeyed; she also knew we needed to get Mary Sue home as quickly as we could. So when they left, she said she went into the living room and sat down to try to think of what to do next…and the tears just came out. And then, Jackson, she said the strangest thing. She said we did have to talk about what I had done because she wanted me to understand how serious it was—but she did not want me to feel worse about it just because I saw her crying. 'I'm the adult here,' she said, 'and you are not responsible for my emotions.' Mom went on to explain that she didn't want me to think that Elizabeth and I couldn't give her hugs for comfort when she had a bad day—and that she hoped we would continue to do that—she just wanted me to understand that we're not responsible for making sure she felt okay. And then Mom asked me if I understood what she meant."

"Did you?" asked Jackson.

"Well, I told her that I wasn't sure, but perhaps I will when I became a mother. And then she leaned back and laughed! You know, Jackson, sometimes she is hard to understand. But she gave me a hug and told me I was a joy to her, so I knew things were better. But then she became serious again and said, 'Okay, let's talk about what happened this afternoon.'"

"So," said Sophie, "I started at the beginning and told her the *whole* thing—you know—about how we were having such a good time riding our bicycles, and then how we stopped for water, and finally how Andy asked about the side trail. Then I told her that *that* was when I made my first big mistake by saying that stupid thing about our parents not wanting us to go into the '*deeeep and terrible* woods' and that it was probably just an exaggeration because parents will do that just so we won't do something they don't want us to do. You know what, Jackson? We sure can do some silly things when we think we are going to be embarrassed, can't we?"

"Tell me about it," said Jackson. "I did the same thing! I should have stepped up and done what I thought was right, too...but I just kept silent."

"Well, anyway," Sophie continued, "I told her how Andy had used my very words to get us to go into the woods—and how, like dummies, we all just followed! I explained that we became interested in all the different things around us—you know, the old shack, the motorcycle trails, and stuff like that—and how it soon had become an exciting adventure! Time went by so quickly...and then I told her how we stepped into the mud pond and about Mary Sue seeing the snake, and how we all knew it was time to get out of there. I did tell her that I had told everyone that we should never have gone in there and that I was sorry I hadn't said so. And then I just said how sorry I was and how angry I was at myself because I had let myself be talked into going."

"What did your mom do then?" asked Jackson.

"She just sat there for a little bit, and then she hugged me again and asked if I knew the real problem with what I had done. I thought for a minute and then told her I guessed it was that I had disobeyed and then made it worse by going along with what I knew was not right. Mom asked me what I meant by that. I thought for a minute and then said, 'It was a sin!' After that, Mom prayed for me, and then I prayed and asked Jesus to forgive me for disobeying my mother...and now I am forgiven! It's so good to be forgiven, isn't it, Jackson? Everything seems new again."

"Yeah, it is—so that was all?" said Jackson.

"*Noooooooo*—I wish!" exclaimed Sophie. "You know what, Jackson? Mom told me the police had caught some guys using drugs back there! That was one reason our parents didn't want us to go into those woods. She said she probably should have told me but that she didn't want to frighten me. Well, that *really* surprised me! Then she talked about the consequences of what I had done...you won't believe all the things I have to do!"

"Like what?" asked Jackson.

"Like…starting this morning, I had to clean my room—not just well, but *really* well! I had to pick up *everything* and put it all away, then polish all my furniture, and finally vacuum the carpet! After finishing all that, I had to clean out my closet—you know [making her voice sound like the voice she had used in the park], my *deeeep and terrible* closet!"

"My story sounds a lot like yours," Jackson added, "except my dad didn't cry! He just got that *look* on his face, and I knew trouble was coming! I had to clean my room too, but then I had to clean out the *deeeeep and terrible* garbage cans…grossed me out!"

"Well," Sophie replied, "I am certainly not finished! I have to wash the dishes every day for a week! I can't use the dishwasher until it's fixed, so the dishes all get piled in the sink—and then I have all those [with every 'deep' getting longer] *deeeeeep and terrible* dishes to do."

"I'm not finished either," replied Jackson. "You saw me over there! I had to dig out all the *deeeeeeep and terrible* weeds from the flower beds."

Sophie began to giggle as she said, "I wonder how many more [and Jackson joined in] *deeeeeeeep and terrible* things they will have for us to do?"

By this time, they were both laughing, and finally, Jackson said, "At least we can laugh about it!"

They sat there just being quiet for a minute, then Sophie said, "Well, I hope I get better at not worrying about being embarrassed when someone wants me to do something that is wrong. I certainly don't like paying the consequences! But…you know what, Jackson?"

"What?" asked Jackson.

"The part I hate the most is when I felt so guilty because I knew ahead of time that what I was going to do was wrong…and I did it anyway!"

"Yeah, Sophie, I felt that way too," said Jackson. "I hope I can learn how to not be afraid to do the right thing!"

"Elizabeth seems to be pretty good at doing that—I may ask her," said Sophie.

And then she went inside to finish the *deeeeep and terrible* dishes.

What Do You Think?

1. Sophie disobeyed her mother and had to apologize to Mary Sue's mom, clean her room really well, and do the dishes for a week. Do you think Sophie's consequences were too hard, too easy, or appropriate?
2. Can you think of any consequences that might have been better?
3. What is the hardest thing about getting into trouble?
4. What was the hardest thing for Sophie?

Prayer

Review Memory Verse: "My son, do not forget my teaching, but keep my commands in your heart, for they will prolong your life many years and bring you peace and prosperity" (Proverbs 3:1–2, NIV).

SUPPLY LIST FOR ACTIVITY 6

Poster board, markers, decorative items

* * *

Activity 6

This activity is designed to help your family discuss "family and house rules" and the consequences of breaking those rules. A website suggestion is listed below that will help you with ideas for this project. This site includes various kinds of charts that can be downloaded free of charge, or you can develop your own chart. Depending on the age of your children, charts can be very simple or decorated with pictures, comical characters, etc., to emphasize each item. The chart can be made up ahead of time, leaving space to write suggested rules, disciplines, and rewards.

As you start your time together, begin by asking your children what they think about what Sophie, Jackson, and their friends did. Then ask whether they think the consequences Sophie and Jackson received from their parents were appropriate. Explain that you would like them to help you set up a simple chart of family and house rules, including consequences—both discipline and rewards. (Be sure you already have five to eight rules in mind that you think are important.) Keep the rules very simple and encourage your children to make suggestions. Disciplines for not obeying the rules can be listed next to each rule. Rewards for good behavior also can be listed—or you might suggest that rewards be a complete surprise! Having a good attitude should get a very high rating!

Websites:

Google "House Rules for Children" and scroll down. Of these, two excellent suggestions are:

- www.rayfowler.org/eight-great-family-rules (This site gives eight family rules that cover just about everything.)

- wikihow.com/House-Rules-for-Kids (This site gives easily understood rules.)

An Excellent Book:

- *New Skills for Frazzled Parents* by Daniel G. Amen (This book is referred to on the Ray Fowler website.)

Supplies to Make Your Own Chart:

- Posterboard
- Markers
- Colorful stick-ons or other decorative items

Parent's Guide for Chapter 6 Devotional 1: Doing the Right Thing

Emphasis

To encourage children to understand that they can stand up for what is "right," "godly," and "wise" in a situation, even though it might be very hard to do. They will also learn that each time they make the right decision, they become a little stronger and a little more prepared to make the next right decision.

Memory Verse: "My son, do not forget my teaching, but keep my commands in your heart, for they will prolong your life many years and bring you peace and prosperity" (Proverbs 3:1–2, NIV).

Suggested Answers to "What Do You Think?" Questions

1. What do you think of Sophie's sister?

    Elizabeth has courage, is brave, is determined to do the right thing and stand up for what she believes—and is a good role model for Sophie and her friends.

2. Have you been in a situation where it was difficult to do the right or wise thing?

3. Who helps you make wise decisions?

    The Lord is our source of wisdom—and He uses your parents and teachers to help you make good, wise decisions.

Prayer

Review Memory Verse

Chapter 6 Devotional 1: Doing the Right Thing

Elizabeth had just celebrated her sixteenth birthday the month before. Her family had given her a big birthday party, and one of her best presents was being told she could get her driver's license. Now Sophie could go with her to different places, and it was really fun for just the two of them to go together. They were on their way back from the mall one afternoon when a car came up beside them at a stoplight. The girl driving honked her horn and waved to Elizabeth. Elizabeth smiled at her and waved back. Then the light turned green, and Elizabeth drove on. Sophie said, "Who was that, Elizabeth?"

"Her name is Beth," Elizabeth replied, "and she took her driver's license test the same time I did."

"I've never heard you talk about her. Is she a new friend?" Sophie asked.

"I don't know if I would call her a friend…she's more like an acquaintance."

"An acquaintance?" said Sophie. "What does that mean?"

"Well, an acquaintance is someone you have met—like a person in one of your classes at school—someone you know, but for one reason or another, you and that person have not become what you would call *friends*."

"Why wouldn't you become friends? Don't you like her? She just smiled and waved at you."

"Friendship can happen, I think," said Elizabeth, "but it may take a little time."

"But why? What's the big deal?"

"Oh Sophie, with all your *whys*—sometimes you can be too much of a little sister! I'll try to explain. I had seen her occasionally at school and had even talked to her a little. When we would see each other by the lockers, we would talk about the previous class or the next pep rally—stuff like that; we had even talked about getting together to study. That was pretty much it until the day I went with Mom to get my driver's license. Beth was there too, and we talked for a short time while we were waiting for our driver's test results. They told us it would be 15 or 20 minutes until we got our tests back, so we went outside just to have something to do. As soon as we got outside, Beth pulled out a pack of cigarettes and asked me if I'd like one. I thanked her but said that I didn't smoke. She didn't say anything—she just looked at me! As she pulled out a cigarette lighter and lit her cigarette, she said, 'I guess I'm not surprised—you probably wouldn't touch a beer either!' I told her she was right and that the last time I checked, there was still an age limit on drinking alcohol. Beth asked me if I was afraid of getting caught. I told her that my real reason was that I really didn't want to do either one of them. Then she said I would never have any really *cool* friends—to which I replied that I already had many *cool* friends! I told her that I chose my friends because I like them and because they care about me, not because they smoke or drink. Then she laughed at me and accused me of probably being a Christian too. I told her there was no 'probably' about it—that I *am* a Christian! I said that I believe Jesus thinks everyone is *cool*—including her!"

Elizabeth paused and then glanced again at Sophie and said, "She just turned around and walked back inside. I finally went back inside, too; the test scores were ready by then. I said a quick prayer for her and then went over to get my test results. But before Beth left, she surprised me by coming over and saying, 'I'm sorry, Elizabeth; I guess I was really rude. I'll see you around.' Then she turned and walked away. I called after her, 'Thanks, Beth, I'll see you at school.' I've seen her a few times since then, and she's been friendly to me, and I'll continue to be friendly to her. If the time ever comes for us to have a friendship, I want her to understand that I want people to be my friends because of who they are, not because they do certain things or act in certain ways just to be *cool!*"

"Wow!" Sophie said. "That's a really neat story, Elizabeth. I hope I'm that brave when I get to be your age. It's hard to say and do the right thing when you think you will get laughed at or made fun of…I sure messed up with the whole *woods* thing."

"I know, it's a hard lesson to learn…and I haven't always had the courage to do the right thing either. But when I do, it makes me a little bit stronger, and I'm a little more prepared for it the next time it happens."

What Do You Think?

1. What do you think of Sophie's sister?
2. Have you been in a situation where it was difficult to do the right or wise thing?
3. Who helps you make wise decisions?

Prayer

Review Memory Verse: "My son, do not forget my teaching, but keep my commands in your heart, for they will prolong your life many years and bring you peace and prosperity" (Proverbs 3:1–2, NIV).

Parent's Guide for Chapter 6 Devotional 2:
A Lesson Learned!

Emphasis

To help your children understand that, even though they are young, they can learn to "think through" situations and make the right decisions. The lesson they learn will continue to help them during their lives.

Scripture Reading: "As iron sharpens iron, so one man sharpens another" (Proverbs 27:17, NIV).

Suggested Answers to "What Do You Think?" Questions

1. Jackson and Sophie were both surprised that they so easily disobeyed their parents. Have you ever felt that way? What could they have done to stop the situation?

They both knew going into the woods was wrong and could have talked to each other and refused to go. They also could have suggested riding to another place on the trail that might have been just as exciting.

2. Jackson seems to have thought through what had happened and come up with a way he could have stopped it from happening. Do you think his solution was a good one? Why?

    Yes, because he would have been doing the right thing by obeying his parents, who had nothing against riding all the way to the end of the bicycle path and, therefore, must have had a good reason for telling them not to go into the woods.

3. "Iron sharpens iron" means that you can help someone do the right thing. What does this mean for you? How can family members help "sharpen" each other?

    Remind your brothers and sisters to obey your parents. Help them learn and understand what is right and what is wrong. Really encourage them when they make good decisions. Also, you can practice having a good attitude as you accept reminders and help from your parents and from your brothers and sisters.

Prayer

Review Memory Verse: "My son, do not forget my teaching, but keep my commands in your heart, for they will prolong your life many years and bring you peace and prosperity" (Proverbs 3:1–2, NIV).

Chapter 6 Devotional 2: A Lesson Learned!

Scripture Reading: "As iron sharpens iron, so one man sharpens another" (Proverbs 27:17, NIV).

"I need to run to the store, Jackson," said his dad. "Would you like to come along?"

"Sure, Dad—I'll be through here in just a minute." Jackson had been emptying all the trash cans in the house and had one more to put in the garbage cans outside. He was excited that his dad had asked him to go with him; he had been doing chores for the last hour and a half. He finished the last one and ran and jumped in the car with his dad.

"All done?" said his dad.

"Yes—I just took the last can outside. Thanks for asking me to go along," replied Jackson.

"Well" Dad said, "you have been steadily working this last hour or so, and you do have school tomorrow, so I thought you might enjoy a break."

"Thanks!" Jackson paused for a moment and then looked at his dad. "I really am sorry for the whole *bicycle/woods* thing! I guess it was just easier to go along with Andy; I'm really embarrassed now."

"Why is that?" asked his dad.

"Well," Jackson continued, "I just know that I didn't have any plans to go into the woods. Andy made it all seem so exciting and said there was no harm in it and that you all were exaggerating about what was back there. It was just a lot easier to *disobey* than I thought it would be! Andy's not a bad kid, Dad…I wonder if he was just showing off in front of Sophie; he kind of likes her! Anyway, I fell right in with him. We've done lots of things together, and this has never happened before. I guess I know now that I wasn't a very good friend to him by agreeing with him about going into the woods."

"Why do you think you weren't a good friend?" encouraged his dad.

"I think a good friend would have done the right thing and told him that if our parents were afraid for us…maybe there was a good reason! That might have helped him to change his mind."

Jackson's dad inwardly breathed a prayer of thanksgiving. They had just pulled into the parking lot at the sporting goods store. He parked the car and then turned to Jackson.

"I'm proud of you, son!"

"You are?" Jason exclaimed. "I thought you would be ashamed of me!"

"Jackson…we all sin…we all fail…and we all bear the consequences of failure. The greatest shame is when we don't learn from our mistakes! You, however, have thought this through and have come to some really good conclusions."

"Thanks, Dad! I just hope I do better if something like this happens again," replied Jackson.

"You know—your comment about being a good friend reminds me of a proverb that goes like this, 'As iron sharpens iron, so one man sharpens another.' Do you know what that means?"

"Well, I know that a knife made of iron will sharpen another knife," said Jackson.

"That's right," replied his dad. And a man who is strong in character and teaches and encourages his friend to be strong is like a sharpened iron knife that will sharpen another knife."

"That's way cool," said Jackson.

Jackson's dad laughed as he opened the car door. "Yes, it is, but your mother is *not* going to think we are *way cool* if we are late for dinner! Let's get what I need and head back home."

What Do You Think?

1. Jackson and Sophie were both surprised that they so easily disobeyed their parents. Have you ever felt that way? What could they have done to stop the situation?
2. Jackson seems to have thought through what had happened and come up with a way he could have stopped it from happening. Do you think his solution was a good one? Why?
3. "Iron sharpens iron" means that you can help someone do the right thing. What does this mean for you? How can family members help "sharpen" each other?

Prayer

Review Memory Verse: "My son, do not forget my teaching, but keep my commands in your heart, for they will prolong your life many years and bring you peace and prosperity" (Proverbs 3:1–2, NIV).

Parent's Guide for Chapter 6 Devotional 3: Wisdom from Aunt Kikky

Emphasis

Jesus illustrated the importance of obedience through the parable of a father and his two sons. Both sons were asked by their father to go to work in the father's vineyard. The answers and actions of the two sons are quite different; they demonstrate both that our actions matter more than our words and that we obey because we trust and respect the one who asked us to obey—whether we want to or not!

Scripture Reading: "Listen to advice and accept discipline, and in the end you will be counted among the wise" (Proverbs 19:20, NIV).

Suggested Answers to "What Do You Think?" Questions

1. Had you heard the parable of the two sons before today? Do you know anyone like either of these two brothers?

   As you listen to the answers, you will learn something about your child's friends. You might also use this opportunity to share your own answer.

2. Do you ever get angry at your mom or dad? What can you do about it?

   Explain that anger is a God-given emotion. The Bible tells us to be angry about things that damage God's reputation and when we see things being done that we know are wrong. But also explain that anger is good for identifying a problem but never good for solving a problem. Good suggestions for dealing with your anger are to talk to your parents about your anger and ask for help with your anger.

3. How can we get rid of bad attitudes?

   This is a tough one for children <u>and</u> adults. A good place to start is <u>wanting</u> to have a heart that wants good attitudes. God gives us parents to help us learn things like this.

   There are many websites that will help parents understand these issues and provide excellent advice and ways of helping their families.

   I have listed two that are biblically based and deal with many types of circumstances, attitudes, and behaviors:

   biblicalparenting.org and christianparenting.org.

   One of the articles on these websites states that attitudes are learned from hearing poor conversations from the media—including music—and from copying the attitudes of friends. It also states that identifying the attitude you want to change is the first step. For instance, a parent would want to change their child's attitude from disrespect to respect and from a demanding attitude to being considerate.

   Both of these websites give biblical answers and help with many questions.

Prayer

Review Memory Verse: "My son, do not forget my teaching, but keep my commands in your heart, for they will prolong your life many years and bring you peace and prosperity" (Proverbs 3:1–2, NIV).

Chapter 6 Devotional 3: Wisdom from Aunt Kikky

Scripture Reading: "Listen to advice and accept instruction, and at the end you will be counted among the wise" (Proverbs 19:20, NIV).

Sophie broke the silence, "Aunt Kikky?"

"Yes?" Sophie's aunt replied.

"Yesterday, while I was cleaning up my room, I began to really wonder about something," said Sophie. She and Elizabeth had gone to Aunt Kikky's house after school the day before and had spent the night because their mom had gone to a conference. Elizabeth had gone to work at her part-time job, and everyone else was gone, too, so she and Aunt Kikky were having a cup of hot chocolate together.

"And what were you wondering about this time?" asked her aunt.

"Well…I didn't like it because I had to clean up my room! I knew Mom was leaving, so I thought that since she wasn't going to be home, it wouldn't hurt for me to wait to clean it up until tomorrow when she comes back. But she said I needed to clean my room right then, so I did…but I didn't like it!"

"And that made you wonder about something?" questioned her aunt.

"Well…sorta," Sophie continued, "I *was* mad, but I tried not to show it…and I was just wondering if that was kind of like…lying?"

"Ahhhh," said Aunt Kikky, "you do come up with some good things to wonder about!"

"Really, Aunt Kikky? Elizabeth says she gets tired of my *wondering* all the time."

"I think that's rather *normal* for a sister who has a busy life," replied her aunt, "but it's still a good question. You said you cleaned your room, didn't you?"

"Yes," said Sophie, "but I sure didn't want to!"

"How did you feel after you finished?" asked her aunt.

"Oh, I was glad it was done, and I wasn't mad anymore! I just didn't think Mom should have asked me to do it right then; after all, I had plenty of time to do it! I *was* glad I finished my room before I came over here. But I was sorry I got angry about it."

"Let me ask you another question. Are you glad it's done so you don't have to go home early to do it?"

"Oh yes, Aunt Kikky—I can sleep later in the morning."

"You think maybe your mother might have known that?" Aunt Kikky asked.

"Hmmm…she probably did—I never thought about that," replied Sophie.

"You know, this reminds me of the parable Jesus told about the man who asked his two sons to work in his fields."

"I don't think I know about that one," said Sophie.

"Well…one day, a father asked one of his two sons to work in his vineyard," began Aunt Kikky. "The son told him *no*—but later, he was sorry he had said no and went to work in the vineyard anyway. The next day, the father asked his second son to work in his vineyard. That son told his father that he would, but then he didn't go! Jesus was trying to teach us that our *actions* do make a difference! You see, saying 'I will obey' *and then doing it* is the only way we can be truly obedient! You didn't want to do what your mom asked you to do, but you went ahead and did it anyway…I think God is pleased with that kind of obedience…"

Sophie interrupted, "But I did have a bad attitude about it."

"I understand," replied her aunt. "None of us enjoy doing things we don't want to do, and that can make us have a bad attitude. But when we *do* obey and experience how good obeying makes us feel, it's a little easier to obey the next time. Then we ask the Lord to forgive us for our bad attitudes and to help us have good attitudes. After that, we just try to continue to be obedient! Does that help you a little bit?"

"Yes, it does—and I did ask Jesus to forgive me last night…when I was missing my mom. But do you know what else I was wondering this morning?"

Aunt Kikky smiled and said, "No. What else were you wondering this morning?"

"I was just wondering why I really like my family—even if Elizabeth *does* get frustrated with me at times."

This time Aunt Kikky laughed and said, "Yes, we are blessed, aren't we…and getting frustrated with family is sometimes just part of life!"

"I guess you're right," said Sophie. "Aunt Kikky, my marshmallows are all gone—do you think I could have some more hot chocolate?"

Aunt Kikky smiled and thought to herself, *I think that means she's ready to change the subject! Thank You, Lord, for Your guidance and care for this special little girl.* She poured two more cups of hot chocolate with marshmallows.

What Do You Think?

1. Had you heard the parable of the two sons before today? Do you know anyone like either of these two brothers?
2. Do you ever get angry at your mom or dad? What can you do about it?
3. How can we get rid of bad attitudes?

Prayer

Review Memory Verse: "My son, do not forget my teaching, but keep my commands in your heart, for they will prolong your life many years and bring you peace and prosperity" (Proverbs 3:1–2, NIV).

CHAPTER 7:
Lies and Ugly Words

Parent's Guide for Chapter 7: Lies and Ugly Words

Emphasis

Sophie finds out that her friend has lied to her, and she is deeply hurt…and angry! Chapter Seven deals with the effects of lying, the fear of trusting her friend again, and the choices Sophie faces. Sophie learns that she must deal with her friend but also work on her own willingness to forgive.

Memory Verse: "Do not say, 'I will repay evil'; wait for the Lord, and He will deliver you" (Proverbs 20:22, ESV).

Suggested Answers to "What Do You Think?" Questions

1. Has someone ever hurt you like Sophie's friend hurt her? Did you want to hurt them back?

2. What are some things we can do when we feel that way?

    Ask the Lord to help you respond the way He would. Talk to your mom or dad and get their advice. Understand that it is very normal to be sad and even angry when someone hurts you.

3. What do you think helped Sophie the most when she was angry and also sad?

    Her mom was there, and she listened to Sophie. Her mom understood how very hurt she was and comforted her.

Prayer

Review Memory Verse: "Do not say, 'I will repay evil'; wait for the Lord, and He will deliver you" (Proverbs 20:22, ESV).

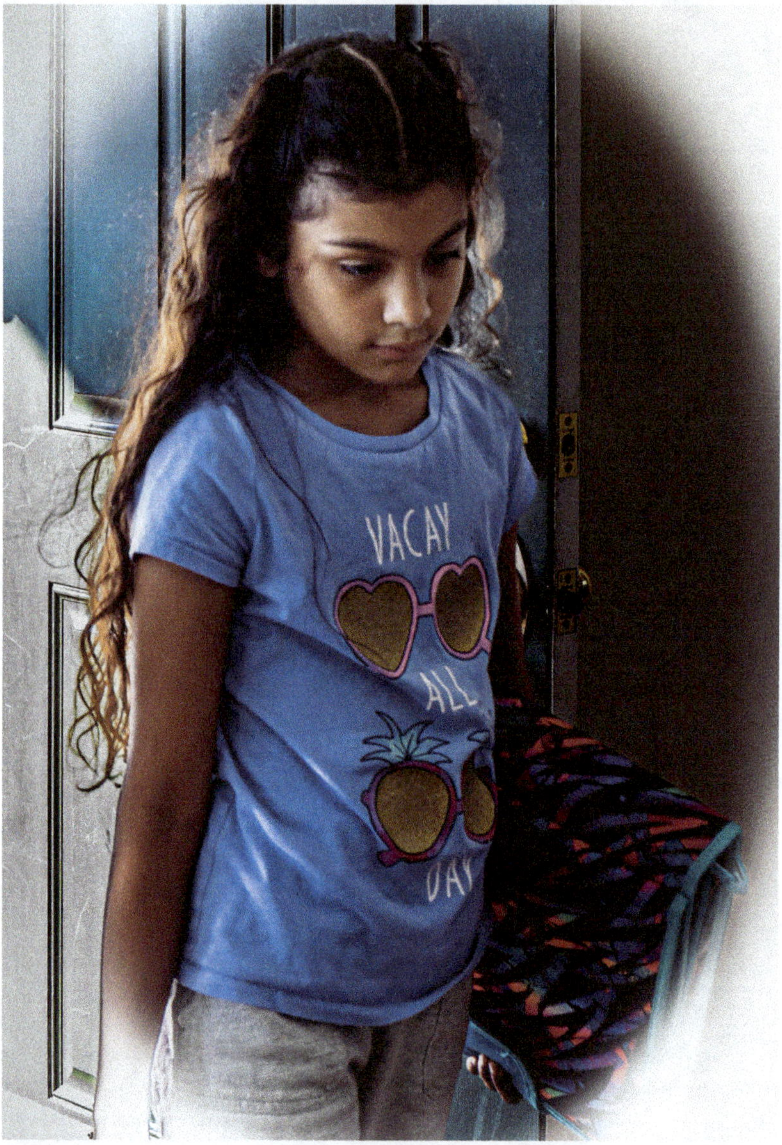
VACAY

Chapter Seven:
Lies and Ugly Words

Sophie slammed the door as she came into the house. "*Mom!*" she called. She was so angry that tears were running down her face.

"*Mom!*" she called again. "*Where are you?*"

"Sophie? Is that you?" Her mother came running into the room. "What's wrong? What has happened?"

"She *lied* to me, Mom—she *lied* to me!"

Sophie's mom breathed a sigh of relief that Sophie wasn't hurt physically and came over and gave her a hug. "Well, come over here, and let's sit down." She got some tissues on the way to the couch, gave them to Sophie, and they sat down on the sofa.

"Now," her mom said, "tell me what happened."

"Well," Sophie sniffed, "you know Betsy and I have been planning for her to spend the night with me this Friday."

"Yes," said her mom.

"We had it all planned. She was coming over after school, we were going to ride bikes and then play Barbies—and we had manicures planned, and we were going to watch movies, and then on Saturday morning, we were going to go shopping at the mall."

"Yes, we've discussed all of that. What has happened?"

"Well, she came to school today and said she couldn't come. When I asked her why, she said her mom wouldn't let her because she had too many chores to do on Saturday. I was really disappointed, but I told her it was okay and that we would plan it another time."

"That was a good way to handle it…so…what is wrong?"

"I was walking to the bus after school, and I saw Betsy with the new girl at school. They had their backs to me and didn't see me, so I was going to say 'hi' to them, but when I got close enough, I heard Betsy say, 'Okay, I'll see you early Saturday morning. We are going to have so much fun!' And then Betsy saw me and got all embarrassed. I didn't know what to say, but I blurted out, 'Where are you going?' And the new girl—her name is Sissy—said, 'Oh, we're going to Water World for the day. Maybe you can come next time, Sophie; I can only take one guest at a time.' I didn't know what to say, Mom! I knew Sissy didn't know anything about Betsy's plans with me, so I just told her that I thought that would be a lot of fun. I looked at Betsy, but she wouldn't even look at me, so I just got on the bus and came home. I found myself getting angrier and angrier—but now I don't feel angry, I'm…I'm…I'm just so sad, and I hurt on the inside, Mom. I just don't understand! Why would Betsy do that? It was mean, and I thought we were such good friends." And Sophie dissolved into tears again.

Sophie's mom wrapped her arms around Sophie and said, "I'm so sorry, Sophie. I know this really hurts. I guess we're not surprised so much when someone we don't know very well hurts us, but when it's one of our good friends, that's another story. I'm not going to try to excuse Betsy—it was really wrong for her to lie to you. I think she probably doesn't get to go to Water World very often, and when the invitation came, she wasn't strong enough to turn it down because she had other plans. And it's okay for you to be angry with her…and very sad. You wouldn't be normal if you didn't feel that way. Those feelings may last for a little while, but then you have some decisions to make."

"What do you mean?"

"Well…what do you want to happen?"

"I don't know…I guess I will have to think about it. I would like for things to be the way they were, but I'm really angry with Betsy—and sad too. How can I believe anything she tells me anymore?"

"Those are all things that you need to think about. Why don't we pray about it and ask Jesus to help you."

So Sophie's mom prayed for Sophie, asking the Lord to protect her from being so angry that she couldn't pray about what had happened and to help Sophie see how she might handle the situation. When she finished praying, she said to Sophie, "I'm going to write down a few things for you. Why don't you read them and think about them, and then we'll talk again about how to handle this, okay?"

"Okay, Mom, but I'm not sure I want to be friends with her anymore!"

"I understand, but read what I'm going to give you and think about it."

Sophie went to the kitchen and got a snack, and then she went to her room to do her homework. Sophie's mom breathed a prayer asking the Lord to help her and thanking Him that she was home early today because of her doctor's appointment. Then she grabbed some paper and a pen and wrote down several thoughts and then several verses from the Book of Proverbs. She thought about what she had written and then took another piece of paper and wrote down just a few that she felt really applied to the situation. She folded the paper and went to give it to Sophie.

"Here, Sophie, read what I've written down and think about it. When you're ready, we'll talk about it, okay?"

"Okay, Mom." Sophie took the paper, laid it down on her bed, and continued to do her homework. But it wasn't long before her curiosity got the better of her, and she picked up the paper and began to read what her mom had written:

"The soothing tongue is a tree of life, but a perverse tongue crushes the spirit" (Proverbs 15:4, NIV).

I'm not sure what that means, thought Sophie, *but something inside me feels...not right!*

"The Lord detests lying lips, but He delights in people who are trustworthy" (Proverbs 12:22, NIV).

"Whoa!" exclaimed Sophie. "God detests lying—that sounds really bad!"

"A hot-tempered person stirs up conflict, but the one who is patient calms a quarrel" (Proverbs 15:18, NIV).

Sophie thought for a minute, *I wonder if I am hot-tempered. I'll have to ask Mom—but I do know I'm angry!*

"Do not say, 'I will repay evil'; wait for the Lord, and He will deliver you" (Proverbs 20:22, ESV).

Sophie thought about this a moment. She didn't know what she was going to do, but she knew she still cared about Betsy, and she didn't want to hurt her back. She wasn't sure how the Lord would help her, but she admitted to herself that she needed help. "Perhaps Mom can help me understand it," she murmured to herself. "But I wonder if I could be mad for just a little while longer!"

After dinner, though, Sophie knew she wasn't angry anymore—she just felt sad. So after she and Elizabeth cleaned up the kitchen, she went looking for her mom and found her in her room, getting her clothes ready for work the next day.

"Mom, could we talk about the list now?" asked Sophie.

"Sure," replied her mom. "Did you bring it with you?"

Sophie pulled it out of her pocket, and they sat down to look at it together. "Some of it I understand," said Sophie, "but there are other parts of it I just don't get. Like in the first one—'The soothing tongue is a tree of life, but a perverse tongue crushes the spirit.' I think the first part means that when we speak gently to people, it makes them feel good—but I'm not really sure what *crushes the spirit* means. Is that why I feel so yucky on the inside?" asked Sophie.

"Yes, it is. When someone says or does something unkind to us, it makes us feel like something is wrong inside of us. That's because we are made in the image of God, so to our spirit inside of us, being lied to is a little like being crushed. And it hurts!"

"Yes, it does hurt!" replied Sophie. "Okay…what about the verse that says God detests lying lips? That sounds really bad!"

"Well…it *is* bad! 'Detest' means disgust or hatred; God is pretty specific here in how *He* views lying. It doesn't mean He won't forgive us, but He does know how hard it will be to trust that person again—and how lying can destroy a relationship. But remember, He delights—or is so happy—when we are faithful to Him and refuse to lie. What do you think about the third one, 'A hot-tempered person stirs up conflict, but the one who is patient calms a quarrel' [Proverbs 15:18, NIV]?"

Sophie thought for a minute and then said, "It makes me wonder if I am hot-tempered! Do you think I am, Mom?"

"No, Sophie, I don't think so. You get angry over things just like all of us do, but you are not one who has an angry spirit. You don't walk around angry all the time like 'hot-tempered' people seem to do."

"Whew! That's a relief!" said Sophie. "When I think about what happened at school today, I get angry all over again…but mostly…I'm just sad."

"The last verse is interesting, isn't it, Sophie, "Do not say, 'I will repay evil'; wait for the Lord, and He will deliver you," Mom read.

"Does that mean I'm supposed to act like it never happened and just trust Betsy like I did before?"

"Not exactly, Sophie. It means that when you forgive her, you can then wait on the Lord because you know that He is going to help you with this friendship. It means that the Lord will help you continue to love her. But Betsy needs to do some things, too. She needs to apologize for lying to you! When she does, the Lord will help you give Betsy time to prove she can be trusted again. And it *may take some time*. When trust has been broken, it just takes a while to trust that person again. That is the really difficult result of lying to someone! That's also why it is so important to never let *lying* become part of our lives."

"Okay, I think I really do forgive her! But I still feel so sad about the whole thing. I'm glad I can count on God's help! He did say He would, didn't He, Mom?"

"Yes, He did!" replied her mom, "and we can wait on Him because we know that He will do what He has promised!"

Memory Verse: "Do not say 'I will repay evil'; wait for the Lord, and He will deliver you" (Proverbs 20:22, ESV).

What Do You Think?

1. Has someone ever hurt you like Sophie's friend hurt her? Did you want to hurt them back?
2. What are some things we can do when we feel that way?
3. What do you think helped Sophie the most when she was angry and also sad?

Prayer

Review Memory Verse

SUPPLY LIST FOR ACTIVITY 7

A clear small drinking glass, a can of Coke, and a few plastic buttons

* * *

Activity 7

This activity involves three object lessons designed to help children understand the damage that can be done when ugly words and lies have been spoken—either by them or about them. Sometimes we are quick to say "I'm sorry" because it's so easy...like after we bump into someone or accidentally spill a glass of water. But even when we are deeply sorry for what we have said—or very forgiving to someone who has lied to us or said something ugly about us—to erase ugly words or hurtful lies from our minds is much more difficult!

Object Lessons:

These are easily prepared object lessons and will be more effective if you do all three on the same day.

Object Lesson #1: Lies Revealed

Supplies:

A clear small drinking glass

A can of Coke

A few plastic buttons

Directions:

Explain to your children that the buttons represent lies or some other sin that we don't want anyone to know about. We think we can hide them, but lies and sins have a way of becoming known.

Pour about four ounces of Coke into the glass. As you drop several buttons into the Coke, tell them that one button represents a lie that has been told; two other buttons represent ugly words that have been spoken to a friend or family member, etc. Point out that the buttons are sinking to the bottom of the glass (but after a few seconds, the buttons will rise to the top again.) Explain to them that most of the things that we *think* are hidden will not be hidden for very long. Remind them that we all fail and sin and that the Bible says, "If we confess our sins, He is faithful and just and will forgive us our sins and purify us from all unrighteousness" (1 John 1:9, NIV). And just like the buttons can be removed (remove buttons), our hearts can be clean again.

Object Lesson #2: Results of Lies and Ugly Words

Supplies (With Close Supervision):

A small ax (to make a gash in a tree trunk)

And/or a suitable knife (to make an initial in a tree)

Directions:

Take your children outside to a tree in your yard. Depending on their ages, let each child put his or her initials in the tree and/or make a small gash in the tree trunk. (If your children are too young, you may have to do this for them.) Tell your children that once the gash or the initials have been cut into the tree trunk, those marks will never go away. Explain that even if they were to come back to this tree in twenty years, these markings would still be there. Tell them that is the way ugly words and lies can affect us. Even when we forgive, it is only God's grace that will help us *forget* some of those words!

Object Lesson #3: Easy Out—Difficult In!

Supplies:

Plastic tablecloth (or use a kitchen counter/table that can be wiped off)

Small tube of toothpaste (travel-sized)—one for each child

Directions:

Part 1—Ask your children to squeeze their toothpaste tubes and make a long line of toothpaste on the table. Tell them the line can be straight or curly—that they can even make a design or a flower. When they have finished and with as stern a face as you can muster, tell them that you want them to scrape up all the toothpaste and put it back into the tube. Naturally, this will cause much frustration as they begin to realize that it can't be done. Then tell them that they are correct—there is absolutely no way to get the toothpaste back into the tube! Explain that once lies or ugly words come out of your mouth, either to someone or about someone, you can never take those words back again! You may *hope* your words will be forgotten, but even though you are truly sorry for what you have said and have even asked for forgiveness, it is only God's grace that will help a person forget those words.

Part 2—The second part of this object lesson is for the parent (who will represent Jesus) to clean up the mess. It is important for children to sit silently and watch the parent clean it all up. Then the parent should say something like, "Because I love you so very much, I choose often to clean up some of your mess; and when it is just toothpaste, I can do that. But the toothpaste I just cleaned up represents the lies and ugly words that all of us have said at one time or another. And no matter how much I love you…I can't clean that up for you or for me! But we have a wonderful Savior who *can* clean up our *mess!* Do you know who that wonderful Savior is? [*Give children time to answer.*] Yes—only Jesus can do that! Just like I cleaned up every bit of the toothpaste even though *you* made the mess, Jesus cleans up all the sins in our hearts—even though *we* made the mess. However, we must remember that even though Jesus forgives us and cleanses us from all our sins, it is much harder for people to whom we have lied or said ugly words to forget our words. Just like those marks on the tree, our *words* last for a very long time! So let's pray and ask Jesus to help us remain silent when we are tempted to say lies or ugly words."

Memory Verse: "Do not say, 'I will repay evil'; wait for the Lord, and He will deliver you" (Proverbs 20:22, ESV).

Parent's Guide for Chapter 7 Devotional 1: Losing Trust

Emphasis

This devotional shows how hard it is to trust someone after that person has lied to you or failed you in some way. It also explains how being irresponsible (not doing what you said you would do) can create a big problem for the one who is depending on you…and it is the same as lying!

Scripture Reading: "Truthful lips endure forever, but a lying tongue lasts only a moment" (Proverbs 12:19, ESV).

Suggested Answers to "What Do You Think?" Questions

1. In this chapter, Sophie's friend lies to her, and Sophie accidentally finds out about it. In Jackson's situation, he found out his friend had lied to others about him. Which do you think would be the most upsetting and hurtful?

   Both are very upsetting and very hurtful, but lying to other people about you is probably more difficult because you don't know how many people have been told the lie.

2. Sometimes people who lie or say ugly words about you do not apologize. What do you do then?

   Ask Jesus to help you forgive that person because Jesus forgave you!

It would not be wise to trust that person again until you both have talked about what was said and the person has apologized to you.

3. If you promise someone you will do something and then don't do it, is this the same as lying?

   Yes! Being deceitful is just a quiet way of lying!

Prayer

Review Memory Verse: "Do not say, 'I will repay evil'; wait for the Lord, and He will deliver you" (Proverbs 20:22, ESV).

Chapter 7 Devotional 1: Losing Trust

Scripture Reading: "Truthful lips endure forever, but a lying tongue lasts only a moment" (Proverbs 12:19, ESV).

"Do you have your science project done, Jackson?" asked Sophie. She and Jackson were waiting in the car for Jackson's dad to take them to school.

"No, it's a volcano eruption project, and it takes two people. I had a friend who was working with me, and I thought everything was going well, but then I had to get someone else."

"What do you mean?" asked Sophie.

"Well, my friend kept telling me he had finished some things, but when we got together, he had barely started on the project. It *really* put us behind, but he said he would have the volcano frame done in two days. We were supposed to meet again last Monday, but he didn't show up."

"That's awful, Jackson—it's due in just two weeks," said Sophie.

"I know, so I talked to Dad about it. He suggested that I call my friend and ask if he had finished the frame. If he hadn't worked on it, Dad said that maybe I should get someone else."

"What happened?" asked Sophie. "Did he get the work done?"

"No! When I called him, he said he needed another two days, so I told him I couldn't wait any longer and would have to get someone else to work with me. He didn't say much, so I think he was mad at me. Then I called Spencer, who was really excited about helping me because his experiment wasn't working out. We've been working on the volcano project ever since."

"It must have been hard to ask someone else," replied Sophie.

"It really was, Sophie, and then I found out later that my first friend, who said he wanted to do the project, was *really* angry about it."

"How did you find out?" asked Sophie.

"His mom called my dad, saying that I had made it hard on her son!"

"Oh, Jackson…I'm so sorry! What did your dad do?"

"He explained to her what had happened, and she understood…but that didn't stop her son from telling my friends at school that I had lied about it."

"Well," said Sophie angrily, "I just wonder about kids who would do something like that! Tell me who it is, and I will go tell him you would *never* lie about it!"

Jackson laughed and said, "Sophie, you and your wondering…but I *was* angry at first. I talked about it with Mom and Dad, and they said that *truth* has a way of coming out, and they were right! I guess he lied about some other things because he got in trouble at school. Then a few days ago, he called and apologized to me for the things he said—and he still wanted to help me with the experiment."

"Are you going to let him?" Sophie asked.

"No…it's too late, but even if it weren't, I would be too afraid he might do the same thing again."

"Yeah, I know!" said Sophie. "I had someone lie to me recently, and it really hurt my feelings; I have forgiven her, but it has been hard to know how to treat her. My mom says it takes time to trust someone after they have lied to you. You *want* to trust them, but you just are not sure they mean what they say."

"That's what my mom and dad said, too," said Jackson. "My mom and dad and your mom think a lot alike, don't they?"

"They sure do!" Sophie replied. "I wonder…"

"No time for wondering now—here comes Dad!"

"I guess you're right," said Sophie. "Hi, Uncle Mike."

What Do You Think?

1. In this chapter, Sophie's friend lies to her, and Sophie accidentally finds out about it. In Jackson's situation, he found out his friend had lied to others about him. Which do you think would be the hardest to handle?
2. Sometimes people who lie or say ugly words about you do not apologize. What do you do then?
4. If you promise someone you will do something and then don't do it, is this the same as lying?

Prayer

Review Memory Verse: "Do not say, 'I will repay evil'; wait for the Lord, and He will deliver you" (Proverbs 20:22, ESV).

Parent's Guide for Chapter 7 Devotional 2: Aunt Kikky's Story

Emphasis

Aunt Kikky shares a story with Sophie about how she once lied to a good friend. She explains how difficult it was to regain the friendship and trust of her friend.

Scripture Reading: "The words of the reckless pierce like swords, but the tongue of the wise brings healing" (Proverbs 12:18, NIV).

Suggested Answers to "What Do You Think?" Questions

1. Can you remember a time when you lied or did something wrong? How did you feel when you knew you were forgiven for what you did?

2. Sophie was shocked that her Aunt Kikky had lied to a friend. How do you think hearing Aunt Kikky's story helped Sophie?

   It was good for Sophie to know that adults also make mistakes and can say that they made a mistake and also learn from their mistakes.

3. What does "reckless words pierce like a sword" mean?

   When a sword cuts you, it is painful—just like ugly words cause pain by hurting your feelings.

4. What does "but the tongue of the wise brings healing" mean?

   Finding someone who listens, understands, and gives wise advice or having someone apologize to you helps take away the pain.

Prayer

Review Memory Verse: "Do not say, 'I will repay evil'; wait for the Lord, and He will deliver you" (Proverbs 20:22, ESV).

Chapter 7 Devotional 2: Aunt Kikky's Story

Scripture Reading: "The words of the reckless pierce like swords, but the tongue of the wise brings healing" (Proverbs 12:18, NIV).

"Good morning, Aunt Kikky," said Sophie.

"Good morning to you, Sophie!" replied her aunt. "You're out early this morning, especially for a Saturday morning. I came out on the deck to enjoy my hot chocolate. Would you like some?"

"I sure would," said Sophie. "Mom wanted me to ask you if she could borrow a cup of sugar; she's making cookies and didn't have quite enough."

"Sure, Sophie, come on inside while I get the sugar, and I'll pour you a cup of chocolate; then we'll come back out here and enjoy the early morning sun together…unless you have to get right back."

"I can stay for a few minutes; Mom said she would get her room cleaned up while I was gone. Do you have any marshmallows?"

"Sure I do," replied her aunt. Sophie followed her aunt into the kitchen and helped set her hot chocolate on a tray. Then they walked back out onto the deck to enjoy their hot drinks.

"How was your week?" asked Aunt Kikky.

"Well, to be honest, it was kind of hard," replied Sophie.

"Why is that?"

"One of my friends lied to me, and I had a hard time with it," replied Sophie.

"Oh! That *is* hard."

"Yes, it really has been hard! Mom helped me a lot, and I do feel a little better. Did you ever have a good friend lie to you, Aunt Kikky?"

"I had worse than that, Sophie! Once *I* lied to a really good friend of mine."

"Oh, Aunt Kikky, you didn't!"

"Yes, I'm ashamed to say I did—and it taught me a valuable lesson," replied Aunt Kikky.

"It did? What was that?"

"I learned that it takes a long time to gain trust back from someone to whom you have lied! Oh—I apologized soon after I lied, and she forgave me…but it definitely put a strain on our friendship that lasted for several months. After I apologized, I just kept being very truthful to her, trying to be extra kind to her and doing things with her when we could. And she did forgive me when I apologized…but it took a long time to regain her trust. Needless to say, I was very careful after that to try and always be honest with my friends."

"I'm glad you told me, Aunt Kikky. You know, I have often wondered why it's always so much fun to be around you and Uncle Mike, and now I think I know why!"

"Why, thank you! And just what answer did your wondering bring?"

"Well, I think it's because you understand us, and you remember what it was like to be a kid! I know that was a really long time ago, but still…you and Uncle Mike have good memories!"

Aunt Kikky laughed and said, "Yes, it was a (really) long time ago, and our memories are still good, but mostly, we just love you and Elizabeth and your mom very much!"

"And we love you too! I think I better go—Mom will have her room cleaned up by now. Thanks for the hot chocolate and for the story. Love you, Aunt Kikky! See you later."

What Do You Think?

1. Can you remember a time when you lied or did something wrong? How did you feel when you knew you were forgiven?
2. Sophie was shocked that her Aunt Kikky had lied to a friend. How do you think hearing Aunt Kikky's story helped Sophie?
3. What does "reckless words pierce like a sword" mean?
4. What does "but the tongue of the wise brings healing" mean?

Prayer

Review Memory Verse: "Do not say, 'I will repay evil'; wait for the Lord, and He will deliver you" (Proverbs 20:22, ESV).

Parent's Guide for Chapter 7 Devotional 3: Growing Up

Emphasis

Since Sophie and her friends often hear adults say to them, "When you grow up," Sophie decides to ask her mom to explain what "growing up" means. Her mom gives Sophie some examples of growing up—or developing maturity—but assures her that everyone, regardless of age, is hurt when a good friend lies to them.

Scripture Reading: "The human spirit is the lamp of the Lord that sheds light on one's inmost being" (Proverbs 20:27, NIV).

What Do You Think?

1. Have you ever been told, "When you grow up, you will understand"? How did that make you feel?

   Like I'm a baby, stupid, frustrated, bad…

2. Sophie's mom tells her that part of being "grown up or mature" is not giving in to what you want "right now." Is this hard just for children?

   Absolutely not! Children may have a hard time resisting a Snickers bar, but adults may have a hard time resisting a new car, new clothes, or a new piece of furniture. Both need to think about saving money and spending money wisely.

3. Her mom also tells her that part of growing up is "having the attitude that you want to follow God's ways, even when you're not sure you really want to." What does that mean to you?

   When your mom tells you to clean your room, take out the trash, or clean the bathroom, and you don't want to, you can choose to obey because you want to please God—and you can choose to have a good attitude as you obey. God loves you however you feel—even when you are angry—but He knows obedience will bring the very best for you.

4. Your scripture reading talks about the lamp of the Lord searching your inmost being. What is your inmost being, and who is doing the searching?

   The Holy Spirit is searching your heart! Do you see how special you are to Jesus when His "lamp" sees the honesty of your heart because you really do want to follow His ways with a good attitude, even though sometimes you don't? God knows your heart, and He also understands your weaknesses. When you do fail—and we all do sometimes—just ask Jesus to forgive you...and start all over again!

Prayer

Review Memory Verse: "Do not say 'I will repay evil'; wait for the Lord, and He will deliver you" (Proverbs 20:22, ESV).

Chapter 7 Devotional 3: Growing Up

Scripture Reading: "The human spirit is the lamp of the Lord that sheds light on one's inmost being" (Proverbs 20:27, NIV).

"Mom?"

"Yes, Sophie?"

"What does it mean to grow up?"

Sophie's mom looked at Sophie and thought to herself, *Dear Jesus, how do I answer this one?* Then she said, "What makes you wonder about this?"

"Well…you know, kids hear a lot of things—like 'when you grow up, you'll know how to do that,' or 'some things you just won't understand until you're grown up,' or 'you're too young to go on that trip,' things like that."

"Yes," replied her mom, "children *do* hear things like that quite often. Sometimes adults just don't know how to answer some of your questions, so they take the easy way and try to put off answering until…"

"Do adults really do that?" Sophie interrupted.

Smiling, Sophie's mom said, "Yes, we can really do that—but perhaps I can explain growing up best by giving you a few examples. For instance, growing up can mean you can be trusted to do what you say you will do or finish a job you have been given to do or use your money wisely…"

"Oh…you mean like not spending my allowance all at once?"

"Yes," continued her mom. "Learning to think about how you want to spend it or perhaps saving most of it for a few weeks so you can have something of value. When you can do that, you are developing self-control and patience because you are not giving in to what you want *right now* but waiting for something better. Growing up is not just about *doing the right things*. Often it's just having the attitude that you want to follow God's ways, even when you're not sure you really want to! Sometimes that involves controlling our anger and learning how to see a problem from another person's point of view."

"That's a lot of stuff!" Sophie said.

"Yes, that *is* a lot of stuff," replied her mom, "and there are many other examples too. Some people grow up quicker than others; also, you can be mature or *grown up* in some areas and immature or *not so grown up* in others. It really does take time. Are you worried about this?"

Sophie thought for a moment and then said, "No, I don't think so. I guess I've been thinking about it because of Betsy lying to me. I'm okay about it now! I just hope we can still be friends. I was thinking today that if I were grown up, maybe it wouldn't have hurt so much."

"No! When a good friend makes that kind of mistake, it always hurts, no matter how old we are. But a big step in growing up is when you can respond to those hurts by forgiving the person who hurt you and by asking Jesus to show you how to love someone even when they might not deserve it."

"And Jesus helps us do that, doesn't He, Mom?"

"Always, Sophie...*Always!*"

What Do You Think?

1. Have you ever been told, "When you grow up, you will understand"?

2. Sophie's mom tells Sophie that part of being "grown-up" or "mature" is not giving in to what you want *right now* but waiting for something better. Do you think this is hard just for children?

3. Sophie's mom also tells her that growing up is sometimes "having the attitude that you want to follow God's ways, even when you're not sure you really want to." Your scripture reading says God's lamp shines on your inmost being (on your heart). If your heart really wants to follow God's ways—and God looks into your heart and sees that—can you understand how happy that makes God and how special you are to Him…even if you're not sure you *want* to do a particular thing?

4. Your scripture reading talks about the lamp of the Lord searching your inmost being. What is your inmost being, and who is doing the searching?

Prayer

Review Memory Verse: "Do not say, 'I will repay evil'; wait for the Lord, and He will deliver you" (Proverbs 20:22, ESV).

CHAPTER 8:
Forgiveness and Grace

Parent's Guide for Chapter 8: Forgiveness and Grace

Emphasis

Sophie begins to understand the power of forgiveness as she reads a story about an amazing little girl named Jazelle, who learned how to forgive in the middle of great sorrow. It is during this time that she gets a call from her friend, Betsy, who asks Sophie to forgive her for the way she treated her. Sophie realizes that her memory verse from the week before is very true and that God would—and did—help her in times of trouble.

Memory Verse: "He holds success in store for the upright; He is a shield to those whose walk is blameless" (Proverbs 2:7, NIV).

Suggested Answers to "What Do You Think?" Questions

1. Have you ever had a friend who has had great sadness in his or her life? Perhaps your friend's sadness is not as deep a sadness as Jazelle's, but it is still very painful.

   Children can relate to this story for many reasons. They may have friends who have:

   - *Lost a loved one through death;*
   - *Lost a loved one through divorce and are now living in a single-parent home—having lost not only a parent but life as they had always known it;*

- *Been or still are very sick or have had serious accidents requiring a long time to heal.*

    The story and this question provide an opportunity for you to listen as your children not only talk about their friends…but also talk about the pain they may be experiencing. It gives you an opportunity to comfort them and assure them that the Lord knows all about their situations, that the Lord will never leave them, and that the Lord will help them just as He had helped Sophie.

2. After Sophie's friend called, what were your thoughts about Betsy?

    She was sorry she had lied; she understood how her not telling the truth had affected Sophie; she was thankful that Sophie would give her another chance to be her friend.

3. How did Sophie react to Betsy's call?

    She was very happy; she realized that it was the Lord who had helped her—just as He had promised He would; she recalled the memory verse from the week before.

Prayer

Before praying, take this opportunity to discuss how we can't always understand the things that happen to our friends or to us, but we can know that the Lord *does* understand every situation and that we can *trust* Him to help us. Then pray with your children, thanking God for your home and family.

Review Memory Verse: "He holds success in store for the upright; He is a shield to those whose walk is blameless" (Proverbs 2:7, NIV).

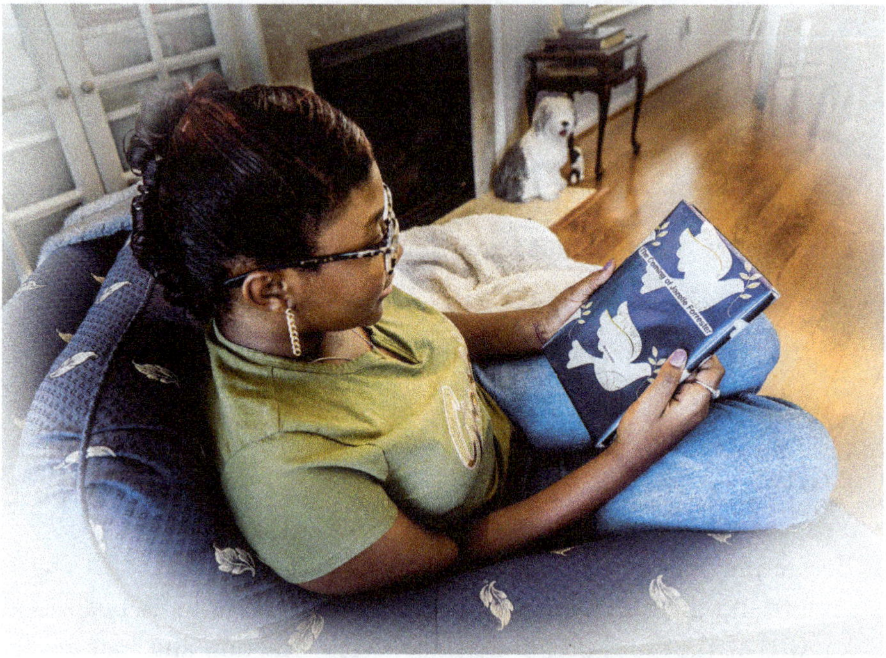

Chapter Eight: Forgiveness and Grace

It was Sunday afternoon, and all was quiet in Sophie's home. After church, Sophie, Elizabeth, and their mom came home, ate leftover lasagna from Saturday night, and cleaned up the kitchen; then, everyone went to their rooms. Sophie was reading a new book, *The Coming of Jazelle Forrester*, that her mom had ordered for her, and it was a *good* book. It was about a little girl named Jazelle who had come from Africa to live in the United States. She had been adopted by American parents and was struggling to adjust to all the new ways of living. The hardest part so far was learning the English language. She had been taught English in her African school and understood it fairly well, but speaking it was much harder. Jazelle's friend, Abby, who lived in the house next door, was helping Jazelle learn English. They were in the same class at school and in just a few weeks they had become good friends and did many things together. It wasn't long before Abby realized that Jazelle had lived through many hard times in Africa. One day when Jazelle was visiting her, Abby began to show her some of their family pictures; but when she looked over at Jazelle to tell her something, Jazelle was crying! Frightened, Abby asked her what was wrong. Jazelle, through tears, told her how her mom and dad died in one of the raids by the warring people of Africa and how very much she missed them and how looking at the pictures made her remember some of the good times she experienced with her parents at home in Africa.

Sophie laid the book down and thought to herself, *I learned about some of this at school when I had to do current event stories in Social Studies, but it felt like I was just reading another story. Reading about someone it really happened to is kind of scary. There must be a lot of children like Jazelle...*

Sophie picked up the book and continued reading. In the story, Abby is horrified at what had happened to Jazelle...*I would have been horrified, too*, thought Sophie...and then Abby told Jazelle how sorry she was that Jazelle had lost her parents. Abby was surprised, however, when Jazelle wiped her tears away and looked up at Abby, and said, "Thank you, Abby! I still miss them very much, and for a long time, I hated the people who caused them to die. But one day, I remembered something my African dad used to say to me over and over, 'Hate destroys, Jazelle—always remember...hate destroys! To forgive our enemies...*that* is our hope!'"

Sophie laid the book down again and thought and wondered...and thought and wondered. Then she went into her mom's room; she was also reading a book.

"Mom?" said Sophie.

"Yes, hon?"

"Have you read this book you gave me about Jazelle and Abby?" Sophie questioned.

"Ahhh...you are reading *The Coming of Jazelle Forrester*...and yes, I have read it. At first, I wasn't sure it was age-appropriate for you, but..."

"What does that mean?" interrupted Sophie.

"It means, among other things, that parents want their children to read books that will challenge them, but at the same time not trouble them or cause them to fear," replied her mom.

"Fear?" Sophie thought for a minute and then said, "Oh—you mean like Jazelle's parents who died in the story!"

"Exactly!" said her mom. "But I decided that since you had studied some current events that were similar to what happened to Jazelle, it was probably okay, especially after I read the book and realized what an amazing little girl Jazelle was."

"She really *was* amazing! I was just reading the part where Jazelle tells her friend, Abby, how her parents died. That was really sad. But then she tells about her African dad, who had taught her that hate destroys and that forgiving their enemies was their hope...I think I'll go read some more."

"Okay, Sophie," replied her mom.

Sophie went back to her room and started reading where she had left off. In the story, Jazelle began to tell Abby about many of her experiences—how she ran away after her parents died, how she found some other children who were also alone, and how they began to go from village to village hoping to find a place to live, how sometimes they were so hungry and struggled to find food, how they were constantly afraid they would be caught by the soldiers, and finally how they came to another small village and found some missionaries who were teaching a class of children right out in the open. The missionaries asked the children to join them and soon realized the children were orphans from one of the destroyed villages. Jazelle tells her friend, Abby, "We were really afraid to trust them, but when they began to talk about Jesus, I knew they were kind people because my mom and dad loved Jesus." Jazelle went on to tell Abby how the missionaries had taken them in, fed and clothed them, taught them each day, and how, after many months, they had found Christian moms and dads for them. "And that," said Jazelle, "is how I came to the United States!" Abby was shocked at what had happened to Jazelle and continued to ask her questions about her adventures. But finally, Abby stopped and said, "Can you really forgive those awful people who did all those things to your family?" And Jazelle answered, "Yes—because that was when I remembered what my dad had told me about how hate destroys. Also, the missionaries helped me understand that it was okay to hate what evil people do, but when we hate the people, it's just like our hate ties us to them like a rope…and I didn't want that to happen! It was very hard, but when I was able to forgive them, my nightmares began to go away, and I realized that I had happy places inside me once again."

Wow! Sophie thought to herself…but her thoughts were interrupted by the ringing of the telephone. "I'll get it," she yelled as she ran into the kitchen and picked up the phone.

"Hello?" Sophie said.

"Hi, Sophie, this is Betsy."

"Oh…hello, Betsy," Sophie replied.

"Can I talk to you for a little bit?" asked Betsy.

"Yes, I guess so," said Sophie.

"Well…" Betsy paused for a moment, "I just called to apologize, Sophie. I know I did a terrible thing when I lied to you about coming to your house. I felt really bad about it, and I know it was wrong. I guess when Sissy called and asked me to go to Water World, I wanted to go really bad, and I was so excited that I just forgot about our plans until she hung up. Then I remembered we had made plans and thought up that stupid thing about having chores to do."

Sophie didn't know what to say, so she just said, "Okay."

"But," Betsy continued, "I felt so guilty about it! When I got home, my mom knew something was wrong, so I finally told her what I had done. She was really upset with me, not just because I had lied but also because I had lied to a good friend. She reminded me that lying is a sin, and I told her I knew that and that I was so ashamed of what I had done. So she prayed with me, and I asked Jesus to forgive me. Then mom asked me what else I needed to do…and I knew what she was thinking…I had to call you and talk to you about it. It took a while before I could get up enough courage…but that's why I'm calling. I am so sorry for lying to you, Sophie; it was terribly wrong! Can you forgive me?"

Sophie was quiet for a moment, and then she said, "Yes, Betsy, I forgive you."

"Do you think we can still be friends?" asked Betsy.

"I think so…I was really mad at you at first, but mostly…I was just so sad about it. You really hurt my feelings! I want us to be friends like we were…but that may take some time."

"That's what my mom told me," said Betsy. "She said it may take some time for you to trust me again."

"Well…I'll talk to my mom, and maybe we can plan something soon, but it won't be as exciting as Water World! Was it really fun?"

"I didn't go," said Betsy.

"You didn't go! Why?"

"My mom wouldn't let me go because I lied to you! So I didn't get to go to Water World, *and* I didn't get to come to your house and do all the things we were going to do. It was a dull, dull weekend! But that's okay, Sophie—I'm going to do my best to make you believe you can trust me again…I'm just glad you have forgiven me!"

"I've done some dumb things too, Betsy! Did I ever tell you about the time I went into the *deep and terrible* woods? It's a long story, and I'll tell you sometime. Thanks for calling me and telling me about what happened. I've been reading a really good book this afternoon. It's about an African girl named Jazelle who was able to forgive people who had done some terrible things! Having a friend lie to me was hard, but it was a small thing compared to what happened to her."

"What happened to her?" asked Betsy.

"Well, it's a really, really long story, and I haven't finished it yet," replied Sophie, "but if you'd like to read it, I'll let you borrow the book when I finish reading it."

"Thanks," said Betsy, "I'd like that!"

"Okay—and thanks again for calling. I'll give you a call in a few days."

Sophie hung up the phone just as her mom came into the kitchen. "Who was that?" asked her mom.

"That was Betsy, Mom. She called to apologize for lying to me."

"She did? Oh, that's wonderful," said her mom.

"I know…she told me all about it. She said she felt so guilty about it that when she went home, she told her mom what she had done. They talked about it and prayed about it, and Betsy asked Jesus to forgive her. Then her mom told her she needed to do something else…and that was to call me. She said it took a little while for her to get up her courage to call me. *Mom*, Betsy asked me to forgive her!"

"And what did you say?" asked her mom.

"I told her I would, and then she wanted to know if we could be friends again. I told her I thought so but that it might take a little time. And she understood—*her* mom had told her the same thing! I told her I would talk to you and maybe we could plan something soon. She also said she was going to do her best to make me believe she could be trusted again. Then I told her I was reading a book about someone who had a lot to forgive—you know, about Jazelle—and Betsy said she would like to read it too. Jazelle really did have a lot to forgive, didn't she? I think she was a very wise little girl!"

"I think you're absolutely right!" said her mom. "Jazelle *was* a wise little girl. Have you finished the book?"

"Not quite—I still have a little left to read. I'm glad I had read most of it before Betsy called. It helped me to read about someone who could forgive so much and how she had 'happy places inside again' when she was able to forgive."

"I'm happy for you, too."

"*He* did it, didn't He, Mom?"

Smiling, Sophie's mom said, "He?"

"You know—my memory verse for last week—the part that says, 'Wait on the Lord, and *He* will deliver you.' He did what He said He would do, didn't He?"

"Yes, and He will every time…perhaps not always the way we think He will, but He *always* will!"

Memory Verse: "He holds success in store for the upright; He is a shield to those whose walk is blameless" (Proverbs 2:7, NIV)

What Do You Think?

1. Have you ever had a friend who has had great sadness in his or her life? Perhaps your friend's sadness is not as deep a sadness as Jazelle's, but it is still very painful.
2. After Sophie's friend Betsy called, what were your thoughts about Betsy?
3. How did Sophie react to Betsy's call?

Prayer

Review Memory Verse: "He holds success in store for the upright; He is a shield to those whose walk is blameless" (Proverbs 2:7, NIV).

SUPPLY LIST FOR ACTIVITY 8

Video (found on YouTube) to learn sign language for "Jesus Loves Me"

* * *

Activity 8

Children will be introduced to sign language in this activity. In the story, the children learn about the power of forgiveness and how forgiving others makes "happy places in our hearts." While this chapter is all about the need to forgive others, Sophie realizes that Jesus helped her resolve the issue with Betsy. The chapter ends with Sophie remembering her memory verse, "Wait on the Lord, and He will deliver you."

The hymn "Jesus Loves Me" is a beautiful description of the fact that Jesus loves you, Jesus is always with you, and Jesus can be depended on to help you with anything that troubles you. Learning the sign language of "Jesus Loves Me" is a wonderful way for children to "see" and "feel" the love of Jesus. Listed below are YouTube videos that teach sign language to this song. The hand movements are very simple and easy to learn—so don't panic! You will need to learn the motions first and then teach them to your children. After you and your children have practiced a few times, you all will have fun singing along with the YouTube version. Once your children have learned the song and hand motions, they probably will never forget it and will have fun teaching the song and motions to their friends.

   1. "Jesus Loves Me in American Sign Language," https://www.youtube.com/watch?v=kljvGJPuGFM
This is probably the easiest one to teach. Keep in mind that every word we speak in English is not always "signed" in sign language. For example, the words "the" and "a" may not be signed, as this video demonstrates. The teacher moves very fast, and you will have to watch the video several times in order to learn the different signs.

2. "How to Sign Jesus Loves Me in American Sign Language," https://www.youtube.com/watch?v=4GAn_CM6IU8
The teacher is more explicit in her directions. She also signs each word, including the small words.

Parent's Guide for Chapter 8 Devotional 1: Remember When?

Emphasis

Sophie finishes reading *The Coming of Jazelle Forrester* and then reflects on her day. As she wonders about it all, she begins to see that just like Jesus forgave her, it is Jesus who gives her the ability to forgive others.

Scripture Reading: "For God so loved the world that He gave His one and only Son, that whoever believes in Him shall not perish but have eternal life" (John 3:16, NIV).

Suggested Answers to "What Do You Think?" Questions

1. Sophie did have a good day, didn't she? What do you think was the most special part of her day?

    Resolving the issue with Betsy. Reading the story of Jazelle because it had a great effect on her.

2. Sophie's experience with the book she had read and with forgiving Betsy reminded her of what?

    That when she asked Jesus to forgive her and to come into her heart—He did.

    That Jesus is the one who helped her to forgive Betsy.

3. Have you ever asked Jesus into your heart?

If your children have done this, now is a good time to pray with them, thanking Jesus for His forgiveness and for living in their hearts.

If your children have not done this and you feel they understand and want to ask Jesus into their hearts, the following illustration may help:

Have available three sheets of construction paper in three colors: black, red, and white.

Let them draw a heart on each color and cut them out. Then explain the following:

Black Heart = stands for all the wrong things we think about, the wrong things we do, and the wrong things we say;

Red Heart = stands for the blood of Jesus when He died for us on the cross;

White Heart = stands for the clean heart that has been forgiven and cleansed by Jesus.

Ask your children if they would like to have a white heart by asking Jesus to forgive them for their sins and asking Him into their hearts. You might want to do this with each child individually.

For children who want to do this, ask them to say the words you say as you lead with a simple prayer:

"Jesus, I'm sorry for the things I've done wrong that make You so sad. Please forgive me and come into my heart to live and help me to do what pleases You. Thank You for loving and forgiving me and for Your promise to always be with me. Amen."

If you think your children do not understand and do not want to do this right now, pray with them and thank Jesus for loving them so much.

Additional Help from Focus on the Family

Shirley Porter

www.focusonthefamily.com is an excellent website containing articles that will help parents lead their children to Christ and many topics about helping children grow and cope in today's society.

Prayer

Review Memory Verse: "He holds success in store for the upright; He is a shield to those whose walk is blameless" (Proverbs 2:7, NIV).

Chapter 8 Devotional 1: Remember When?

Scripture Reading: "For God so loved the world that He gave His one and only Son, that whosoever believes in Him shall not perish, but have eternal life" (John 3:16, NIV).

It has been such a good day, Sophie thought as she closed the book *The Coming of Jazelle Forrester*. After church and lunch, she had read most of her book about Jazelle; then Betsy had called, and Sophie had shared the good news with her mom. Elizabeth came in while Sophie and her mom were talking and was so happy for Sophie that her friendship with Betsy was being repaired. Then Sophie went back to her room and finished Jazelle's story. Now, as she closed the book, she lay in bed thinking and wondering about Jazelle and all she had been through. Then her thoughts turned to Betsy and how happy she was that Betsy had called and how they were going to be friends again. After a few minutes, she got up, put on her pajamas, and had just finished brushing her teeth when her mom came into the room.

"Are you ready for bed?" her mom asked.

"Yes—I just finished brushing my teeth." Sophie jumped into bed, and her mom sat down beside her.

"It has been a really good day, hasn't it?"

"Yes, I think we all have had a happy and restful Sunday! Did you finish your book?"

"Yes," Sophie replied. "It was a really good book—I would love to meet Jazelle one day!"

"That *would* be special, wouldn't it!" replied her mom. "And it was really special that Betsy called too, wasn't it?"

"Oh yes, it was! You know—I have been wondering and wondering about all of this."

"*You* have been wondering? Oh my—I am *soooo* surprised!"

"*Mommmm*," replied Sophie.

"I'm just kidding; I love for you to tell me all the things you wonder about! What is it this time?"

"Well, I was thinking about when I gave my heart to Jesus. Do you remember when I did that?"

"I certainly do!" said her mom. "It was a very special time—I won't ever forget that!"

"I was eight years old, wasn't I?" asked Sophie.

"Yes—as I recall, it wasn't long after your eighth birthday. Has something reminded you of that?" asked her mom.

"Well…I was thinking about Jazelle and how she forgave those awful people who caused her parents to die, and then I thought about Betsy calling me and asking me to forgive her and how happy that made me."

"And how did that remind you of when you gave your heart to Jesus?" asked her mom.

"I just think that if I hadn't asked Jesus to come into my heart, I wouldn't have been able to forgive Betsy, and I certainly don't think Jazelle would have been able to forgive and not hate those people who hurt her unless Jesus was in her heart, too!"

"And why is that?"

"Well…I had lots of sins too, but Jesus still loved me and forgave me, and when I asked Him to come into my heart, His Spirit came in to help me follow Him. That's what you told me would happen, and I just think that's what helped me to forgive. *We* have been forgiven, and He helps us to love and forgive others. Isn't that true?"

"Yes, that is very true. One of my favorite scriptures comes from the Gospel of John…I think it's in the thirteenth chapter where Jesus says,

'A new command I give you: Love one another. As I have loved you, so you must love one another.' When we ask Him to live in our hearts, He helps us to love other people and gives us the desire and strength to forgive people when they hurt us."

"Jesus forgave me with all my sins, Mom, and I have to do the same thing…forgive people when they hurt me!" said Sophie.

"Those are excellent thoughts! Hmmm…I think I see really sleepy eyes. I guess it must be time to go to sleep. Would *you* like to pray tonight?"

"Okay." Sophie closed her eyes and prayed, "Dear Jesus, thank You for helping me with my friend, Betsy. I know You have so much to do, but You said You would help, and You did—and I thank You. And I don't know Jazelle except through the book I read about her, but I thank You for helping her learn all about forgiving even really mean and bad people 'cause I think she helps all of us who read her story. I love having *happy places in my heart*, and I know they are there because You have forgiven me, and You live in my heart. Good night."

Sophie opened her eyes and said, "Good night, Mom—I love you, and I'll see you in the morning."

"Good night, and I love you, too!" And as Sophie's mom turned out the light and left the room, she also breathed a prayer of praise to the Lord, who has forgiven so much for so many people and who helps His people to forgive others.

Scripture Reading: "I love those who love me, and those who seek me find me" (Proverbs 8:17, NIV).

"For God so loved the world that He gave His one and only Son, that whoever believes in Him shall not perish but have eternal life" (John 3:16, NIV).

What Do You Think?

1. Sophie *did* have a good day, didn't she? What do you think was the most special part of her day?
2. Sophie's experience with the book she had read and with forgiving Betsy reminded her of what?
3. Have you ever asked Jesus into your heart?

Prayer

Review Memory Verse: "He holds success in store for the upright; He is a shield to those whose walk is blameless" (Proverbs 2:7, NIV).

Parent's Guide for Chapter 8 Devotional 2: My Bike Was Stolen!

Emphasis

This devotional comes from a true story about a little boy whose bike was stolen. The story shows the tender heart of someone who, even though terribly wronged, was willing to forgive and wanted whoever stole his bike to know that he had forgiven him. In doing so, the guilty person not only returned his bike but repaired it as well. Sometimes when we make choices to do the right thing, God brings an instant blessing. God does not always work this way, but when He does, it is a joyous occasion and a tremendous confidence builder of one's faith.

Scripture Reading: "Blessings are on the head of the righteous, but the mouth of the wicked conceals violence" (Proverbs 10:6, ESV).

Suggested Answers to "What Do You Think?" Questions

1. Have you ever had something stolen, or do you know of someone who had something stolen?

    If they have, ask them how it made them feel. If they have not, perhaps you have, or perhaps you know of someone who has. A real-life example might help them relate to this story.

1. What did you think about Joshua?

    Unbelievable—lots of wisdom for a young person

2. Why do you think he chose to forgive?

   Because Jesus forgave him of all the things he had done wrong and still forgives him—it was the right thing to do.

3. Do you think you could forgive this kind of wrong?

   Certainly, it should be our desire to forgive. Remind them that Joshua had been taught about forgiveness and its blessings, but he still had to "choose" to act on what he had learned. He could have just become really angry and focused on his loss.

4. Does God always answer our prayers this way?

   Sometimes He does, but not always! (God isn't a snack machine who always answers just like we want…but…He always answers…and the answers are always for our good: sometimes "yes," sometimes "no," sometimes "not now/wait.") When we are obedient to how God wants us to live, God gives us His peace, and we feel good about doing the right thing. Having His peace when things go wrong helps us know for sure that God is with us.

Prayer

Review Memory Verse: "He holds success in store for the upright; He is a shield to those whose walk is blameless" (Proverbs 2:7, NIV).

Chapter 8 Devotional 2: My Bike Was Stolen!*

Scripture Reading: "Blessings are on the head of the righteous, but the mouth of the wicked conceals violence" (Proverbs 10:6, ESV).

"Hi, Sophie," Jackson called as he was coming out of his house. Sophie was in the flower garden cutting some flowers off the rose bushes to put in a vase for company that was coming.

"Hey, Jackson. What's up?"

Jackson walked over to where Sophie was. "Did you hear about Joshua?"

"You mean Joshua Hendrix in the next block?"

"That's the one," said Jackson. "He had his bike stolen last week!"

"Oh no!" exclaimed Sophie. "He loved that bike!"

"Yes, he did, but you will never believe what happened."

Sophie laughed and said, "Well, try me!"

"Okay! Joshua was coming out of his house one day last week—I think he said it was Tuesday—and he saw a man loading his bike into his car. Joshua shouted at him, but the man drove off with his bike."

"Oh, that's so sad! I will have to call him and tell him how sorry I am."

"*Noooo*. You can call him and congratulate him!"

"Jackson—that's mean! I'm not going to do that!" Sophie exclaimed.

"Well, just wait till you hear the rest of the story! Our teacher said Joshua has strong faith, and he told his dad that he forgave the thief, but he wanted the thief to know it. So his dad bought a large piece of poster board, and Joshua wrote on it and then stapled it to a sawhorse."

"What's a sawhorse?" interrupted Sophie.

"Sophie, sometimes *I wonder* about *you*! A sawhorse is something carpenters use. It's sort of like a trestle or frame that they build so that they will have something to support wood that they want to saw."

"Hmmm," said Sophie, "I wonder why they call it a *sawhorse*."

Jackson just looked at her and said, "Can we just get back to the story?"

"Okay, so what happened?" asked Sophie.

"Well, this is what he wrote on the poster board:

'To the person who stole my bike:

You really hurt my feelings when you took my bike.

But I am a Christian, and because Jesus forgave me,

I FORGIVE YOU!'"

"Isn't that something?" Jackson said to Sophie.

"That *is* amazing!" replied Sophie. "Is it still there?"

"Nope—when Joshua's dad left for work the next morning, the sign was face down in the yard…and over in the driveway, the bike was back—*and* it had new handlebars and grips and a new front fork unit."

Sophie just stared in shock at Jackson. "Wow! That *really is* amazing! That's something Joshua will never forget. I don't think we will ever forget it, either! Thanks for telling me; I'm going in to tell Mom. See you later!"

"See ya, don't forget the soccer game tomorrow; we're in a tie for first place."

"We won't forget—see you then."

What Do You Think?

1. Have you ever had something stolen, or do you know of someone who has had something stolen?
2. What did you think about Joshua? Why do you think he chose to forgive?
3. Do you think you could forgive this kind of wrong?
4. Does God always answer our prayers this way?

Prayer

Review Memory Verse: "He holds success in store for the upright; He is a shield to those whose walk is blameless" (Proverbs 2:7, NIV).

Parent's Guide for Chapter 8 Devotional 3: Who Is the Prodigal Son?

Emphasis

The continuing theme of the story of the prodigal son is the power of forgiveness. However, the elder brother is also emphasized as the one who "did all the right things," but because of his jealousy and self-righteous attitude, his heart is as prodigal as his younger brother's heart.

Scripture Reading: "Wisdom's instruction is to fear the Lord, and humility comes before honor" (Proverbs 15:33, NIV).

Suggested Answers to "What Do You Think?" Questions

1. Why do you think the younger son wanted to leave his home?

   Wealthy visitors who talked about riches and entertainment in the cities might have been passing through. He probably didn't have to work because his father had lots of money and servants, so he might have been bored. He was rebellious and wanted to "do his own thing" without obeying any rules or receiving any consequences.

1. Why do you think it bothered the older brother so much when his dad let his younger brother come back home?

   He was jealous of his younger brother because he had stayed home and done what was right, while his younger brother had taken his father's money before he should have and then wasted it! After all that, he felt his father was rewarding his younger brother, who had done wrong, with a party! He might have thought his father loved his younger brother more.

2. What do you think Sophie's mom meant when she said, "Out of the mouths of babes"?

   Sometimes children speak great truths, and they are completely unaware of what they are saying! God uses everyone in the family to help each other...and that includes children, who may say great truths very innocently because God is working in their hearts, also. It is encouraging for children to know that they, too, can be used by God!

Prayer

Review Memory Verse: "He holds success in store for the upright; He is a shield to those whose walk is blameless" (Proverbs 2:7, NIV).

Chapter 8 Devotional 3: Who Is the Prodigal Son?

Scripture Reading: "Wisdom's instruction is to fear the Lord, and humility comes before honor" (Proverbs 15:33, NIV).

"Mom," said Sophie.

"Yes?" replied her mom. They had just returned some books to the library and were now on their way to the Christian bookstore to buy another copy of *The Coming of Jazelle Forrester* for one of Sophie's friends who had moved to another city.

"Do you remember the story of the prodigal son?" asked Sophie.

"Yes, I do; it's a wonderful story!"

"It's in my little devotional book, and I read about him today."

"Why don't you refresh my memory about him?" replied Sophie's mom.

"Well," began Sophie, "it's about a son who wanted his inheritance from his dad—only he wanted it *right now* instead of waiting until after his dad died. *And* he kept on insisting that his dad give it to him… so his dad did! Then the son really made a mess of things because he left home and went off somewhere and spent all his money on *stuff* and on partying. He had lots of friends until his money was gone; then those *friends* didn't want to have anything to do with him."

"He found himself in quite a mess, didn't he!" said her mom. "Then what happened?"

"Well, he finally got work picking up this yucky stuff in pig pens…pea pods…or something like that. But he was so hungry from not eating for a long time that he began to remember how nice it had been at home and how good he had it there. So he told himself that he would go back home and ask his father to forgive him…and also ask his dad if he could just be his servant. That would really be sad, wouldn't it, Mom, to go back to your home and then *not* be part of the family anymore…to just be a servant?"

"Yes, that would be very sad indeed. Is that what he did?" asked her mom.

"Oh, *Mommm*, you know what he did! But do you know what was really great about the story? His father saw him coming when he was still very far away and didn't wait for his son to get to the house. He ran out to meet him and threw his arms around him, and welcomed him home! The son told his dad how sorry he was and then asked his dad to forgive him…he tried to tell his dad that he would be a servant in his house…but his dad ignored what he said and called his servants and told them to prepare a huge feast. Then he put a robe around his son, and they had a big party because his son had come home. I bet it was a great party, don't you think so?"

"Yes, I imagine it was a wonderful party—and it is a great story! It was a very happy time."

"Well…not for everyone!" said Sophie. "His older brother was really angry about how his younger brother was being honored. He complained to his dad, reminding him that *he* had worked for him all his life and had been faithful to help him, and yet his dad hadn't even one time thrown a party for him and his friends."

"That is quite true—his older brother did complain…but remember what his father told his older son, 'You are always with me, and everything I have is yours, but your brother was dead, and now he's alive—so we need to celebrate…'"

"Yes," Sophie interrupted, "but I have been wondering about all of that!" She paused and waited a moment. "Aren't you going to ask me what I wondered?'

Sophie's mom laughed and said, "I thought maybe you would get around to it! So…did you come to any conclusions after you *wondered* for a while?"

"Well, Mom, I was just thinking about the older brother and how angry he got. I can kind of see how he felt; after all, he *had* stayed home and done what his dad wanted him to do. What I really don't understand is why it sounded like he didn't miss his brother at all! You think maybe he was just jealous because his little brother was getting so much attention?"

"I think you have wondered correctly," said her mom. "Jealousy is always an ugly trait!"

"Uh-huh! If you could color jealousy on a piece of paper, I bet it would be an ugly, yucky mud color! I don't want that in *my* heart...but sometimes it can be easy to be jealous when someone else has something you would like to have or gets to do something that you would like to do and can't. I don't want to be like the older brother. When I read about him, I just wondered if maybe *he* was like the *prodigal son*!"

Sophie's mom glanced over at her and thought, *Dear Jesus—out of the mouths of babes!* But then she said, "You are so right! It seems they were both prodigal sons, but the difference between them is that the younger son came back and asked for forgiveness. And *that* is how we know what to do when thoughts of jealousy—or any other sin—come into our lives. We tell Jesus that we are sorry and ask Him to forgive us! And He is just like the father in the story...He readily forgives us and then rejoices with us!"

"Hmmm, that really is great. I hope the older brother asked Jesus—and his father—to forgive him, too...even if that wasn't in the story! Oh, look—there's the store. That didn't take long at all!"

What Do You Think?

1. Why do you think the younger son wanted to leave his home?
1. Why do you think it bothered the older brother so much when his dad let his younger brother come back home?
2. What do you think Sophie's mom meant when she said, "Out of the mouths of babes"?

Prayer

Review Memory Verse: "He holds success in store for the upright; He is a shield to those whose walk is blameless" (Proverbs 2:7, NIV).

CHAPTER 9:
A Shelter in the Storm

Parent's Guide for Chapter 9: A Shelter in the Storm

Emphasis

Sophie talks to her Uncle Mike about her parents' divorce, her lingering questions about why it happened, and her struggles because she misses her dad. Uncle Mike shares the great story of Joseph and the reality of how God uses everything in our lives for our good and for His purpose.

Memory Verse: "The name of the Lord is a fortified tower; the righteous run to it and are safe" (Proverbs 18:10, NIV).

Suggested Answers to "What Do You Think?" Questions

1. Did you remember the story of Joseph? Being sold into slavery is hard for us to imagine, isn't it? What do you think it might be like?

   It is difficult for any of us to imagine, but perhaps you can relate to it by thinking about how hard it would be to stay in one room all day—every day—never being able to play with your friends and having to eat in that room all by yourself.

1. What do you think helped Joseph more than anything else?

   Perhaps he remembered his father telling him stories about how God had taken care of his family in the past. He also knew that staying true to his honesty and trying to do the right thing had gained favor and respect from his jailers and his masters.

2. Does God still help His people today?

    Absolutely! God's promise that He will always work everything in our lives for our good is still true.

Prayer

Review Memory Verse: "The name of the Lord is a fortified tower; the righteous run to it and are safe" (Proverbs 18:10, NIV).

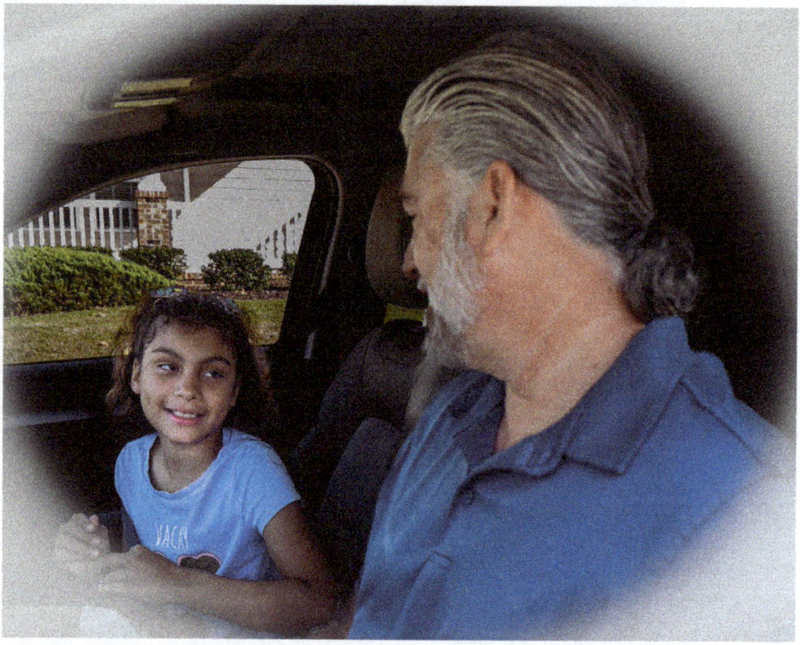

Chapter Nine:
A Shelter in the Storm

Uncle Mike and Sophie were driving back from the airport after seeing Aunt Kikky and Jackson off to visit Aunt Kikky's mom. Aunt Kikky wanted to help her mom as she recovered from a bad case of the flu, and Jackson had also gone along to help. School had been out for a couple of weeks, so Sophie had been spending more time with her aunt and uncle. She loved being at their house—they always made her feel welcome, and she always had a good time. The summer had already been full of fishing trips, reading adventure books, and swimming in their pool—and besides all that, Aunt Kikky was a great cook!

"You're really quiet today, Sophie," said Uncle Mike. "You must be *wondering* about something. Were you sad to see your aunt and Jackson leave?"

"Yes…I'm going to miss them, but I know Aunt Kikky's mom needs her right now—and it's just for a couple of weeks. You think her mom is going to be okay?"

"Oh yes," replied her uncle. "Your aunt had been planning a visit soon anyway, and this way, she can help her mom plus have a good visit. When you get older, you don't bounce back from being sick as quickly as you did when you were younger, so Kikky just wanted to be there. Jackson loves visiting his gramma and gramps, so they'll have a good time…but I will miss them, too!"

Sophie was quiet for a minute, "Uncle Mike?"

"Yes?" he replied.

"You and Aunt Kikky have been married for a long time, haven't you?"

"Yes, I guess you could say that; we've been married for twenty-five years."

"My mom and dad were only married for fifteen years. Do you remember when they got married?"

"I certainly do—it was a happy time for all of us! Is that what you've been thinking about?"

"Uh-huh…It seems like every time I go to an airport, I think of my dad. I guess that's because we don't go to an airport very often, so it reminds me of when Elizabeth and I go to visit him."

"You miss your dad, don't you?"

Sophie sighed and said, "I really do! It's much easier now, but sometimes it just makes me wonder about adults and what they do! When I ask Mom about it, she tries to explain—and I think she really does understand that it still hurts—but that doesn't help me to *not* miss him!"

"He's your dad, hon…it's normal to miss him," replied Uncle Mike.

"That's what Mom says, too. She says when we love someone, it's normal to want to be around them. I guess that means that my mom and dad don't love each other anymore since they don't want to be around each other. How does that work when we are supposed to love everyone?"

"Have you asked your mom about this?" asked Uncle Mike.

"No…most things I can ask my mom about, but for some reason, I just can't ask her about this. Is that wrong?" asked Sophie.

"Oh no," said Uncle Mike. "Some questions are hard to ask, and I can understand how you might have a hard time asking her this one. Let me ask you a question. Do you think your mom was sad when they separated and divorced? You were only six years old at the time, so that may be hard to answer."

"I know I was only six, but I do remember. Mom was really sad for a long time, even though I think she tried to hide it from us 'cause she was always doing something to try and make us laugh."

"And did she succeed?" questioned Uncle Mike.

"Yes…many times she did—and still does! Mom can be lots of fun! But I remember how I used to hear her crying when she didn't know I was listening."

"Did that happen often?" asked Uncle Mike.

"No, not too many times…but I knew she was really sad."

"That must have been hard for you; you were just a little girl."

"It *was* hard…I remember crying a lot, too—but Mom just seemed to know what to say to make me feel better. She's really good at that—and she always prayed for us. Sometimes she, Elizabeth, and I would pray together just about being sad. I can't say those were happy times, but they were…I'm not sure I know how to explain…"

"I think I do," said Uncle Mike. "Maybe they were just…quiet times!"

"Yes—that's just what they were!" Sophie was quiet for a minute and then said, "But Uncle Mike, you didn't answer my question."

"I know, and I didn't forget. You've asked a difficult question, and it doesn't have an easy answer. Let's try to look at it this way…you love your mom and Elizabeth very much, don't you?"

"Oh yes, Uncle Mike—I really do!"

"And you love your dad and Aunt Kikky and me and our family and your nana and papa, right?"

"Yes, of course I do—you all are my family!" Sophie replied.

"Do you love your friends?" asked Uncle Mike.

"Sure I do—but that's different," said Sophie. "I mean…I *do* love them, but I…I don't know, that confuses me! I guess I do love my family more than my friends, but that doesn't sound right, does it?"

"It may not *sound* right to you, but maybe that's because the love you know best is the kind of love that your family has given you. You see, there are lots of different kinds of love. The greatest love we know about is the love God has for us. Then, there is the kind of love that you have for a new puppy and…"

"Oh yes," interrupted Sophie. "I just love your new puppy! He's so cute and cuddly, and he just makes us all so happy, doesn't he?"

Uncle Mike laughed and said, "That is true! He does make us laugh, and he is very cute—and that's another kind of love! Then there's the love we have for our family, the love we have for our friends, the love we have for our country, the love we have for God's beautiful earth… and the love between a man and a woman that makes them want to get married and live together for the rest of their lives—and they do believe that they will love each other and stay married forever! Sometimes, however, life doesn't work out the way we thought it would—and a marriage ends in divorce…like your mom and dad's marriage. If you were to ask them today if they loved each other, I believe they would say *yes—but it's a different kind of love!* When there is a divorce, I think there is always great sorrow in both people…because there were happy times in that marriage, too. For instance, your mom and dad were so happy when Elizabeth was born! Then when they found out you were coming, they were so excited that they called every person they could think of to let them know they were having another child. Plus, they spent lots of time choosing names for you and for your sister! They wanted you both to have names they felt God would choose."

"That's true! Mom told me how they chose my name," said Sophie.

"And they did the same for Elizabeth! They also asked us to pray for you when you were sick, when school was difficult, or when you had disappointments. And they were always taking pictures…"

"Oh yes, we have *soooo* many pictures, and I just love looking at them all! Some of them are really funny; they bring back so many good memories!"

"Do you remember the time we rented a house at the beach, and the whole family went there for a week? You were only four years old at the time."

"Yes, I *do* remember—or at least part of it. What I remember is building a castle in the sand, and then we covered Dad up with sand, and Mom came along and asked us if we had seen him. I know now that she was just pretending—but back then, I thought we had fooled her. It was really funny!" Sophie paused for a minute…and then said, "Those were really happy times…and I guess I just want to have them back."

"I know, Sophie…and that probably is true for every child whose parents have gone through a divorce. Life is sometimes very painful for each one of us! A friend of mine told me something a couple of years ago that might help you—something that you really need to understand."

"What did your friend tell you?"

"Your mom and dad may be divorced from each other…but neither one of them ever divorced you or Elizabeth—and they never will! They both love you so much, and they love spending time with you, watching you grow up, and being involved in your life in all the things you do!"

"Wow, Uncle Mike…I never thought about it like that. I really do know they both love me, even if I don't get to see my dad as much as I would like. Is it still okay to just *wonder why* sometimes?"

"It certainly is! You know, I was thinking about your family this morning while I was reading in the Bible about Joseph. You remember Joseph, don't you?"

"Sure I do!" Sophie remembered because it was one of her favorite stories—so she went full speed ahead, trying to tell the whole story in one breath! "He had a terrible time! His brothers were really mean to him! Do you know that they even sold Joseph as a slave—and then he had to live in a different country—and then he ended up in prison for…how many years?"

"I think it was around fourteen…"

"Yes—and he helped the baker and that other guy—and they were supposed to help him, but they didn't—until the Pharaoh had those terrible dreams—and then they remembered that Joseph could explain dreams—and then he was made ruler next to Pharaoh—and he saved all the people because he knew how to keep enough food—and then his brothers came from way off to buy food, and they didn't even recognize him! When Joseph finally told them who he was, they were really scared, weren't they?"

Uncle Mike grinned. "I would say that just about covers it!"

"Oh no, Uncle Mike—there was *a lot* more! They made up all those excuses and trips so they would go back home and get their youngest brother. But then it all ended really well because Joseph forgave them—and his brothers went and got their dad—and they brought him to Egypt, where Joseph was living—and they all lived there for a really long time! It was a neat story!" Sophie sat back and said, "Whew! I guess I was talking a little fast, wasn't I?"

Uncle Mike laughed and laughed! When he finally caught his breath, he replied, "Yes, Sophie—I think you outdid yourself this time!"

Sophie looked over at him and said, "We were talking about Mom and Dad and the divorce—what does Joseph have to do with that?"

"Good question! Do you remember how frightened Joseph's brothers were when they found out who Joseph was…and do you remember what Joseph said to them in response?"

"Hmmm…not really."

"Joseph told them not to be afraid because what they had meant for evil, God had used for good! Joseph was telling his brothers that even though they were really mean to him, and even though he had suffered for many years because of what they had done to him, God had used all of those experiences for good in Joseph's life. Joseph was only seventeen years old when his brothers sold him as a slave—that's just a year older than your sister; Joseph was thirty-seven years old before he saw his brothers again! I'm sure he *wondered* about many things, just like you do! You see, God had a special plan for Joseph, and over those twenty years, God put him in situations that would train him for that special plan. When the time came for God to use Joseph in that special plan, Joseph not only had the skills needed to save the people of Egypt from starvation—he also saved all the Jews, who were his own people—and his family from starvation. Everyone had enough to eat because of the wisdom Joseph had learned from God! What happened in Joseph's life is a lesson for all of us to learn. God has a plan for your life, too—and He will use even the painful things that happen to you to make your life full of joy and to make you a blessing to others!"

Sophie was quiet again…and finally said, "That's because He loves us, isn't it?"

"Yes, it's because God loves us all! He really is like a strong tower that keeps us safe—and we can always run to Him when we don't understand what is going on in our lives."

"Thanks, Uncle Mike—you've given me a lot of good things to think about! It's so easy to talk to you…maybe that's because I know how much you love my mom!"

"I do, and we love *all of you* very much! Speaking of your mom, she probably expects me to buy you some lunch! I don't know about you, but I'm getting hungry—so let's find a place to eat."

"Great—I'm hungry, too! I'd love a hamburger and fries."

"Sounds good to me! I know a place not too far away that has great ice cream, too!"

"Wow—that would be great!"

What Do You Think?

1. Did you remember the story of Joseph? Being sold into slavery is hard for us to imagine, isn't it? What do you think it might be like?
2. What do you think helped Joseph more than anything else?
3. Does God still help His people today?

Prayer

Review Memory Verse: "The name of the Lord is a fortified tower; the righteous run to it and are safe" (Proverbs 18:10, NIV).

SUPPLY LIST FOR ACTIVITY 9

Object lesson of "The Truth That Holds"—an afghan

* * *

Activity 9

This activity is an object lesson to show the wonderful reality of the truth that God's amazing grace is what holds us in all of life. We often think we must hold tighter to Jesus when life is difficult—as in the reality of divorce, loss, or abuse—and in these times, we do spend more time praying or endeavoring to trust His truths. The wonderful reality, however, is that God holds on tightly to us! It is God's amazing love that holds us and is that tower of strength that hovers all around us and never fails! While this activity can be read as presented, as an object lesson, you may want to tell it in your own words. Any small afghan can be used while explaining "The Truth That Holds." However, an extra measure of understanding would be gained if you could give your children their own special afghan to help them remember this concept.

The Truth That Holds

Sophie had some serious questions for Uncle Mike, didn't she? And like Sophie, many have gone through the experience of having their parents divorce. There are also other very hard things that children go through—like the death of a loved one or a severe illness that either they have had or a loved one has had…or even now may have. When we go through these sad events, we often have questions and find ourselves asking, "Why?" Sometimes we may even think we are going through hard things because we have done something wrong. When we pray and ask God to change things—and things don't change—then it is easy to think that God must not love us or God does not really care.

As Sophie remembered the story about Joseph that her Uncle Mike told her, she remembered what Joseph had said to his brothers when they came to his court. *Do you remember what he said?* [Give them time to answer.] Joseph told them, "Do not be afraid because what you meant as evil, God meant for good, for He has done amazing things." I think it would have been easy for Joseph to doubt God and fear for his safety. And I am sure there were discouraging times when he wondered if God was with him—yet he did not depend on his feelings; Joseph depended on what he knew was the truth! The reality is that when we belong to God, His amazing love holds on to us in any and every part of our lives.

[Pick up the afghan and begin folding it into as small a box shape as you can.] This afghan is going to help me show you, in a small way, just how our safety in our Heavenly Father works when we know His Son, Jesus, who is all truth. When I have finished folding this afghan into a small square, it will look a little like a tiny box. Now I want you to use your imagination and pretend that *all truth* is in this soft, tiny box—that includes everything you know about truth; everything you know about our Heavenly Father, the Holy Spirit, and Jesus; everything you know about love and kindness; everything you know about comfort and good times; all the things you know about honesty and joy; and all the things you know about God's power and might. I want you to pretend all of this knowledge is wrapped up in this folded afghan. Now, hold out your arms so I can place the afghan in your arms, and then I want you to just hold it. [Place the afghan in their outstretched arms.] Now I want you to try to understand that you are holding all the truth of the world in your arms. [Let them hold it for a little bit; then, as you take it from them, unfold it and wrap it around their shoulders as snugly as you can while saying to them something like the following.] But this is the difference. While we can know many truths—and hopefully many more as we learn about Jesus—the great wonder is that when we know Him, it is *His* truth that holds *us* because God is a shield and a strong tower of safety for His children and He preserves and takes care of His own. So while at times we will be frightened or discouraged over things that happen in our lives, it is His truth, awesomeness, and amazing love that holds us! Proverbs 16:3 (NIV) says, "Commit to the Lord whatever you do, and He will establish your plans." And one of the scripture readings we have had before states, "Every word of God is flawless; He is a shield for those who trust in Him." Isn't it wonderful that we serve an amazing God whose magnificent love will hold us all our lives in any and every circumstance just as snugly as this afghan holds you right now? Let's say a prayer and thank God for all that He does and for all He will continue to do in our lives.

Parent's Guide for Chapter 9 Devotional 1: A Good Day!

Emphasis

To help children realize that they are often given great encouragement from people who love them when they let them know they are troubled. To also help children know and understand that they can pray to our Lord, who will give them His words of comfort and joy.

Scripture Reading: "Blessed is the one who finds wisdom, and the one who gets understanding; for the gain from her is better than gain from silver, and her profit better than gold" (Proverbs 3:13–14, ESV).

Suggested Answers to "What Do You Think?" Questions

1. Isn't it good to feel happy for Sophie after she had been so sad the day before?
   Yes. When someone has a problem and is going through a hard time, it is always encouraging to know that answers have been found to help solve the problem.

2. What was it that really made her know it was a good day?
   Sophie realized that after she had prayed, Jesus helped her by showing her He was living within her by giving her "happy places" in her heart and that He is always with her, even in the sad times. Sophie's mom helped her to see that even though she would have sad times again, it was God's way of showing her He would always be with her.

Prayer

Review Memory Verse: "The name of the Lord is a fortified tower; the righteous run to it and are safe" (Proverbs 18:10, NIV).

Chapter 9 Devotional 1: A Good Day!

Scripture Reading: "Blessed is the one who finds wisdom, and the one who finds understanding; for the gain from her is better than the gain from silver; and her profit better than gold" (Proverbs 3:13–14, ESV).

The sun was peeking through the curtains when Sophie awoke, and she lay in bed thinking how really glad she was that it was Saturday and she didn't have to get up early and get dressed to go anywhere. It was quiet in the house, and she stretched and pulled the covers up around her and thought, *It's going to be a good day!* As she lay there thinking about her trip to the airport the day before, she remembered her talk with her Uncle Mike and how at first, she had been afraid to talk to him about her mom and dad. She also thought about how easy and *(she searched for the right word)*...comfortable talking to him had been once she got started! Elizabeth had come over after they had arrived home, and then their mom had come home from work, and after dinner, they went to play miniature golf. Sophie had been really tired by the time they all got home, and it wasn't long before she had gone to her room for the night. Now, as she lay in bed thinking about her conversation with Uncle Mike and about all he had said about the different kinds of love, she began to wonder about all of it.

I know that I am not very wise, she thought, *but I know that Uncle Mike is! When he talks to me about things like this, I just really know that I can trust him and that he is telling me good things—like what he said about Mom and Dad not divorcing us. Maybe I did feel that way a little...I was only six...I can remember wondering what was going to happen to Elizabeth and me. Then there was that part about Joseph when he told his brothers that even though they had meant it for evil, God had meant it for good...I hadn't remembered that! I guess Mom is right again when she says that the enemy of God will always do what he can to make us doubt that God will take care of us—and that's just when we need to trust Him even more!*

Sophie lay there a little bit longer, and then she very softly began to whisper her own little prayer, "Dear Jesus, I know I am just a little girl and that I'm not very good at praying yet at all, but I really like the story about Joseph and how You gave him the courage to be strong when so many bad things happened to him...and You really did make all those things that his brothers meant for evil turn into good things! I don't even know for sure how to pray about my mom and dad getting a divorce, but I do know they love me—and Elizabeth, too—and I know You love my mom...and my dad! So even though I am not sure how to do it, can I just tell You that I do trust You, and I do know that You will be with all of us? Whew—that was a long prayer, Lord...I hope You heard all of it. Amen!"

When Sophie finished, she lay very still for a moment, and then she thought, *Hmmm, for some reason, I sure do have happy places in my heart... and I don't feel sad anymore! What a wonderful thing to wonder about!*

Just about that time, Sophie's mom came into the room and said, "Good morning, dear Sophie! Are you ready for a good day?"

"Yes, Mom—it's already a good day! Want to know why?"

"You know I do." She went over and sat down on Sophie's bed and said, "Okay, so why is today *already* a good day?"

"Well...first, I guess I have to tell you about yesterday when Uncle Mike and I were coming home from the airport. I hope this doesn't make you sad, but when I go to the airport, I nearly always think of Dad...and then I get lonely to see him."

"I can understand that, and I think that Uncle Mike probably knew you were sad, and maybe he tried to help you."

"Mom, sometimes I just wonder about you and Uncle Mike. I don't know how you and my uncle can think so much alike! Anyway...yes, he did know—and so we talked about Dad, and we talked about the divorce, and we talked about me being sad and not understanding some things."

"I think it's wonderful that you can talk to your Uncle Mike about all of those things; some things are probably hard for you to talk about with me."

"See—that's what I mean—Uncle Mike said the exact same thing!"

Sophie's mom smiled and said, "And did he help you?"

"Oh yes, he did! He talked about all the different kinds of love, how you and Dad didn't divorce Elizabeth and me, and about Joseph and all the things that happened to him and how God turned all those things into good blessings. *That* was really amazing!

"I see," replied Sophie's mom, "and I agree—that is all really amazing! So…is that why today is such a good day?"

"Well…sorta…but not *just* that. I finally decided to pray about it—and I did! I told Jesus that I really didn't know how to pray very well, but that I knew He loved all of us and that I didn't know how to do it well, but that I did trust Him and that I knew He would be with all of us."

Sophie's mom was quiet for a moment and then said, "Well, I can certainly see why you would think it's already a good day!"

"That's true, but that wasn't the best thing."

"No? Then what was the best thing?"

"It was when I got through praying, Mom! I just lay here for a little bit, and then all of a sudden, I knew I had happy places in my heart…and I wasn't sad anymore! Isn't that a wonderful thing to wonder about? I just wonder if it's because Jesus lives in my heart, and He's showing me that!"

Sophie's mom laughed with a laugh that was filled with joy!

Joy because she knew in her heart that while all those who loved Sophie could assure her about how God would continue to be with her, it was when Sophie knew for herself personally that Jesus was speaking to her heart that she would find the greatest comfort and assurance. So she leaned over and gave Sophie a big hug and said, "Oh yes, that *is* because Jesus lives in your heart—and that *is* His Holy Spirit telling you that you are going to be just fine! That doesn't mean that you won't ever be sad again or that you won't miss your dad…because you will. But it *does* mean that God will make all things work for good in your life. And yes…I *can* see why it's already a good day!"

Sophie jumped out of bed and said, "Okay—what shall we do first?"

"Well…I thought after breakfast, we might go look at those shoes you were so interested in at the shoe store and then go by the library."

"Oh good," interrupted Sophie, "and I'll come to help you with breakfast!

And together, they walked hand in hand to the kitchen to start their wonderful Saturday.

What Do You Think?

1. Isn't it good to feel happy for Sophie after she had been so sad the day before?
2. What was it that really made her know it was a good day?

Prayer

Review Memory Verse: "The name of the Lord is a fortified tower; the righteous run to it and are safe" (Proverbs 18:10, NIV).

Parent's Guide for Chapter 9 Devotional 2: Completing a Mission

Emphasis

To assure your children that many people have gone through great trials and that God was faithful in using these trials and sufferings to make them strong. When God gives someone a mission, He always supplies the strength and courage to complete it.

Scripture Reading: "Commit to the Lord whatever you do, and He will establish your plans" (Proverbs 16:3, NIV).

Suggested Answers to "What Do You Think?" Questions

1. Had you ever heard of Harriet Tubman?

    After your children answer, you can go over some of the information about her; children learn about her in school, usually by the fifth grade. Harriet Tubman was an African-American believer in Jesus Christ, an abolitionist, a humanitarian, and a Union spy during the American Civil War.

2. Can you see how God used even the really hard things in her life to help her complete her mission?

    God used the pain and abuse she received as a child to strengthen her and prepare her for the hard life she would have in the future. She was an amazing woman who was fearless in the face of opposition as she helped other slaves escape to freedom. God had given her a mission, and she was determined to complete it!

3. Do you know anyone today who has overcome obstacles like Mrs. Tubman?

If they don't, you may have heard about a missionary—or maybe know someone in your family or in your church—who is doing work for God that would seem impossible to your children. Explain to your children that God gives each of us His special strength to complete whatever task He gives us to do—whether it's a difficult task like Harriet Tubman had or carrying out simple responsibilities like cleaning their rooms or cleaning the bathroom. We can always depend on God to give us His grace and to supply our needs!

Prayer

Review Memory Verse: "The name of the Lord is a fortified tower; the righteous run to it and are safe" (Proverbs 18:10, NIV).

Chapter 9 Devotional 2: Completing a Mission

Scripture Reading: "Commit to the Lord whatever you do, and He will establish your plans" (Proverbs 16:3, NIV).

Sophie knocked on Elizabeth's door. "Elizabeth…can I come in?"

"Sure," came the reply.

Sophie entered her room and went over to the desk where Elizabeth was working. "What are you working on?"

"I'm just finishing up a long book report that is due tomorrow. Hang on just a minute." She typed the few remaining words and then said, "There—it's finally done! I'm so glad to have that finished—it was a really long one!"

"What book did you read for your report?" asked Sophie.

"It was a very interesting book about Harriet Tubman."

"Oh…I remember studying about her. Wasn't she the African-American lady who helped slaves escape during the Civil War?" asked Sophie.

"Yes…and she was an *amazing* woman! Some reports said she helped over 300 slaves escape to freedom in the North—that meant she made over nineteen trips from Maryland to southern states and then back to Maryland under extremely dangerous circumstances! Of course, she was a slave, too—she was born a slave in Maryland. So the first thing she had to do was to escape from the people who owned her. She finally escaped all by herself and went north and found work in Pennsylvania and New Jersey. But it wasn't long before Harriet began to go back to Maryland to free other slaves."

"Wow, she must have been very brave!"

"She was, but she had been through some very hard things when she was just a little girl, and God used those hard things to prepare her for the hard life He knew she would have. By the time Harriet was five or six years old, she had to start working. She was beaten many times and passed around from one owner to another because they didn't like her work. Then, when she was twelve years old, one of the slave masters threw a two-pound weight at her, striking her head, because she wouldn't help him tie up a slave who was trying to escape. That head injury caused her to have narcolepsy…"

"Narcolepsy?" interrupted Sophie. "What's that?"

"Well…as I understand it, it's something that happens to your brain that makes you fall asleep at certain times—and you just can't help it," replied Elizabeth.

"You mean she could have fallen asleep at times when she was trying to help people escape?"

"That's right! So you can see how amazing her saving more than 300 slaves really was! Harriet Tubman knew God's purpose for her life was to help slaves become free, and God helped her do just that! She had a strong will and was a very determined woman! She had to be! Many times she had nothing to eat for days; she had to sleep in the woods, and she was always aware that she could be caught and killed—and yet she refused to quit!"

"Oh, Elizabeth," Sophie couldn't help but interrupt again, "she really *was* brave!"

"Yes, she really was. Reading about her life made me wonder if I would have been that brave! Part of the escape route for slaves was through Pennsylvania, which was a *free* state. But many slave owners were angry about what was happening, and eventually, laws were passed to stop people from helping slaves escape to freedom. It was a very dangerous time for Harriet Tubman—and for the slaves she was helping! There were even large rewards offered for her capture—some by slave owners and some because of the laws that were passed. This just made it harder for Harriet and the Underground Railroad…"

"A railroad?" interrupted Sophie again.

"Well…it wasn't *really* a railroad—it just *acted* like a railroad because so many people in so many different states helped *move* the slaves to freedom. Plus, it was all done in secret—like undercover work!"

"Oh—you mean like the mystery stories where the good guys work undercover, so no one knows who they *really* are?" said Sophie.

Elizabeth smiled. "Something like that," she said. "Only it wasn't fiction—this all really happened—and it must have been really scary!"

"So…where were the slaves taken so they could live *free*?" asked Sophie.

"When Pennsylvania became unsafe, there were people all along the way who risked their lives to help Harriet Tubman get the slaves to Canada, where slavery was not allowed!" She even crossed Niagara Falls on a rope suspension bridge with them!"

"I remember seeing Niagara Falls in those movies we watched a few weeks ago," exclaimed Sophie. "I can't even imagine how scary that must have been!"

"I can't either, Sophie—it must have been terrifying—and she did it many, many times! And her work didn't stop there. During the war—and even after the war—Harriet Tubman did so many things to improve the lives of the people she had saved. She raised money for freedmen's schools, she helped orphaned children, and she even transformed her family's home into a home for old people who had no one to care for them."

"You mean she gave up her own home?" asked Sophie. "Wouldn't that be hard to do?"

"I don't think so. I think doing things for other people was such a part of her life that it just became easier and easier. It seems like her whole life became part of the vision that God had given to her…and that she would never give up on! She knew that all the hard times had just made her stronger and more determined to complete her mission.

Wait a second—let me find something she once told a reporter…ahh, here it is: 'Now do you suppose He [God] wanted me to do this just for a day or for a week? No! The Lord who told me to take care of my people meant me to do it just as long as I live, and so I do what He told me to do!'"

"Whoa! She was really something, wasn't she?"

"Yes…she really was. Isn't it amazing that regardless of all the cruel treatment she received, she just knew God was going to use it all to make her strong so she could complete her work?"

"Hmmm…I know it's a whole different story, but Harriet Tubman reminds me of Joseph in the Bible. He was also a slave—and he was in prison when he hadn't done anything wrong—and really bad things happened to him…but he always knew God was with him, too—and in the end, Joseph was able to save the entire nation, plus all the Jewish people!"

"You're right. God used very hard things to prepare both Harriet and Joseph to complete His mission for their lives."

"What a great book report! I bet you get an A on it!"

"Thank you. I hope you're right!"

What Do You Think?

1. Had you ever heard of Harriet Tubman?
2. Can you see how God used even the really hard things to help her complete her mission?
3. Do you know anyone today who has overcome obstacles like Mrs. Tubman?

Prayer

Review Memory Verse: "The name of the Lord is a fortified tower; the righteous run to it and are safe" (Proverbs 18:10, NIV).

Parent's Guide for Chapter 9 Devotional 3: Shining Answers…Like the Morning Sun!

Emphasis

As Sophie, Elizabeth, and their mom have dinner, each one has a particular answer to prayer that they share with each other. This serves as evidence that God does answer our prayers—not always in the way we thought He would, as in the answer to Elizabeth's prayer, but nevertheless, wonderful answers. Answered prayer is definitely a time for us to rejoice and be grateful!

Scripture Reading: "The path of the righteous is like the morning sun, shining ever brighter till the full light of day" (Proverbs 4:18, NIV).

Suggested Answers to "What Do You Think?" Questions

1. Sophie, Elizabeth, and their mom had three wonderful answers to prayer that they shared with each other. Do you have any recent prayers, either in your family or among your friends, that you have prayed for and that you know have been answered?

    If your children cannot think of anything, perhaps you can share some of your answers to prayers or the answers of people you know.

2. Have you ever had to get up really early in the morning as the first little bit of dawn's light came into view? It was still very dark, wasn't it? When you got up, you had to turn on the light to see better; but as the sun got brighter and brighter, you no longer needed the light in your room. The sunlight enabled you to see everything clearly. Your scripture reading says that the "path of the righteous is like the morning sun, shining ever brighter till the full light of day." What do you think this means, and how can we understand this even in the prayers we pray?

When we first begin to walk down the path Jesus has given us, it is often like walking down a path in the woods at the first light of day—we cannot see the path clearly. Just as the sun gets brighter and brighter during the day and the path gets clearer and clearer, the truths in the Bible help us to see and understand God's ways—the paths He wants us to take—and they, too, become clearer and clearer. When we pray and do not receive the answer we want, it's a little like walking down that dark pathway. As we continue to trust God, we will come to see that every prayer of a child of God is always answered—every time! The answers may not always be what we want to hear, and they may not come as fast as we would like—but they always come the right way in God's timing because it is God's way!

Prayer

Review Memory Verse: "The name of the Lord is a fortified tower; the righteous run into it and are safe" (Proverbs 18:10, NIV).

Chapter 9 Devotional 3: Shining Answers…Like the Morning Sun!

It *had* been a good day! Saturdays were almost always good days for Sophie and Elizabeth. Even though there were always extra chores to do, their mom tried really hard to make them interesting. For instance, if they had to dust and polish all the furniture, she would sometimes hide little candy bars or nickels, dimes, and quarters in drawers or under books. These treasures became theirs when the work was completed. One time, when the girls had done an excellent job cleaning the whole house, they picked up their plates after dinner and found movie tickets along with a note that said, "Well done, girls—let's go to a movie!"

The treasures, however, were not always presents or fun things to do. Sometimes their mom would cook a "surprise" *(of course, she wouldn't allow them in the kitchen)*, and when she was finished, they would find out that their favorite foods had been prepared, and they would sit down to a wonderful dinner…and that's what it was today! Sophie loved homemade pizza, and Elizabeth loved warm brownies with ice cream on top—so they all sat down to pizza, a green salad, and a wonderful dessert!

Sophie loved eating dinner with her mom and Elizabeth because they both had so many interesting experiences to share. Her mom nearly always had interesting things happening at work to share, and Elizabeth had so many friends that someone was always doing something fun, getting into trouble, or sometimes just studying a subject she had never heard about.

Tonight, however, was really special because Elizabeth was telling them about her friend's brother, Randy, who had lost the basketball scholarship when he broke his arm. "It was such good news," Elizabeth said. "Do you remember how disappointed Randy was because he had lost his scholarship?

"Oh, I remember," replied Sophie. "We prayed for him—remember? He was really depressed and didn't know what he was going to do about college."

"That's right…he was so discouraged about it," said Elizabeth. "But I think everyone's prayers helped him because he decided he was not going to let it get him down, and he began to put extra time into his studies—including taking some pre-college courses. He had a high average in his studies anyway, but now he has a 4.0, which is as high as you can get…and has received an academic scholarship with full benefits!"

"Oh Elizabeth, that is such good news!" said their mom, "and yes, what a wonderful answer to prayer! It's always so good to hear things like that because it helps us remember that God *does* hear our prayers and *will* work things out for us in wonderful ways."

"We were all really excited about the news…and I think we were all encouraged, too. By the way, Sophie, Mom said you had a great answer to prayer. Does it have anything to do with your visit with Betsy the other day?"

"Yes, it does," said Sophie. "You've been working so many extra hours lately and haven't been home as much, so I'll explain what happened. I know you remember when she apologized for lying to me and wanted us to get together. Well…last Thursday, Betsy and her mom invited me over for lunch. They had prepared a special *friends'* lunch, and I wasn't allowed to help in any way! They had made Key lime pie for dessert…"

"Oh great! Your favorite dessert!" exclaimed Elizabeth.

"Yes—my favorite dessert—and right in the middle of the pie was a candle. As Betsy lit the candle, she told me it was because I was such a special friend and that she wanted me to know again how sorry she was for lying to me. Actually, I had really just kind of forgotten all about it. You know, I wonder about that sometimes…I was really angry with her…but I really had forgotten all about it! Maybe when you really forgive someone, it's much easier to forget the way they hurt you…you think so, Elizabeth?"

"I think you just might be right—and I'm happy for you! That's another big answer to prayer, isn't it?"

"Uh-huh—it sure is!" Sophie replied.

"Well, guess what?" their mom interrupted. "I, too, have a wonderful answer to prayer!"

"What?" both girls asked at the same time.

"I have been praying about my job, hoping that I would soon get a raise…and I did!"

"Yeah!" Sophie and Elizabeth cried as they clapped their hands. "That's great, Mom!"

"Yes, it certainly is! Not only will there be more money in my paycheck, but my boss said I would be able to work from home some of the time—at least two days a week, and soon maybe three!"

"Oh, Mom—that is *soooo* wonderful! It's going to be great to have you home more!" said Sophie, as Elizabeth nodded in agreement.

"Yes, it is," replied their mom. "We just have so much to be thankful for, don't we, girls? Why don't we take a minute and thank the Lord for all the ways He answers prayer…and especially for those we have talked about today."

They bowed their heads while their mom thanked the Lord for all of His goodness—and especially for the prayers that were answered this week, which were so clearly blessings from Him and also great assurances of the way He cares for His people.

Scripture Reading: "The path of the righteous is like the morning sun, shining ever brighter till the full light of day" (Proverbs 4:18, NIV).

What Do You Think?

1. Sophie, Elizabeth, and their mom had three wonderful answers to prayer that they shared with each other. Do you have any recent prayers, either in your family or among your friends, that you have prayed for that you know have been answered?
2. Have you ever had to get up really early in the morning as the first little bit of dawn's light came into view? It was still very dark, wasn't it? When you got up, you had to turn on the light to see better; but as the sun got brighter and brighter, you no longer needed the light in your room. The sunlight enabled you to see everything clearly. Your scripture reading says that the "path of the righteous is like the morning sun, shining ever brighter till the full light of day." What do you think this means, and how can we understand this even in the prayers we pray?

Prayer

Review Memory Verse: "The name of the Lord is a fortified tower; the righteous run to it and are safe" (Proverbs 18:10, NIV).

CHAPTER 10:
Sophie's Dream

Parent's Guide for Chapter 10: Sophie's Dream

Emphasis

Sophie awakens her mother to tell her of a dream that brings to her remembrance a scripture that was on her name poster about being in Jesus, "who became wisdom from God." She tells her mom that since Jesus became wisdom for us and died on the cross for us, maybe it's really important to learn more about what wisdom is. The essence of the chapter is to help children see that, in the final analysis, wisdom is really knowing Jesus, His Father, and the Holy Spirit.

Memory Verse: "Above all else, guard your heart, for everything you do flows from it" (Proverbs 4:23, NIV).

Suggested Answers to "What Do You Think?" Questions

1. Do you dream often? Do you sometimes have dreams that are a little scary? Are you surprised that Sophie would dream about Jesus at the cross?

   These are simple yes and no questions, but let your children elaborate on their dreams and their surprise about Sophie's dream.

2. What do you think of Sophie's dream? Is it scary to you, or do you think it might be one that she will remember for a long time and be a blessing to her?

   Dreams are surprising at times and a riddle that many have thought about, tried to unravel as to their meaning, and even written books about. Dreams were often used in the Bible to explain situations and to give direction for a problem. For instance, Joseph's dreams about the baker and the cupbearer later became the very source of his eventual release. So while dreams, for the most part, are just ways our minds handle the events in our lives when we are sleeping, there certainly can be times when God uses them in special ways to help us see Him more clearly. This is what happened to Sophie, and it is a dream that she will never forget because it helped her to see that Jesus truly did become wisdom for all of us, and in seeking Him, we will find treasures of knowledge, comfort, and direction.

Prayer

Memory Verse: "Above all else, guard your heart, for everything you do flows from it" (Proverbs 4:23, NIV).

Above all else, guard your heart, for everything you do flows from it.

Proverbs 4:23 NIV

Chapter Ten:
Sophie's Dream

Sophie quietly walked down the hall into her mom's room and stood by her bed. "Mom?" Sophie whispered.

"Sophie? Are you okay?" Her mom sat up, looked at the clock, and said, "It's 4:00 o'clock *in the morning!* What's wrong? Are you sick?"

"I don't think so," replied Sophie, "but…could I get in bed with you? I had a dream."

"Okay, hon." She slipped over to make room, and Sophie got into bed with her. As she did, the moonlight coming through the window fell across Sophie's face, and her mom saw tears streaming from her eyes.

"Oh, Sophie…you're crying!" she exclaimed. "Was it a really frightening dream?"

"Well…I guess it was—but not like a monster dream or anything like that."

"You want to tell me about it?"

"Yes…yes, I do," replied Sophie quietly. She remained silent for a little while and then said, "I dreamed I was in a strange land, and there were a lot of people, and they were all wearing different clothes than we wear. I was standing outside on a little hill, and I could see there were even more people way off in the distance, and they were all looking at something; I could hear some of them yelling, and I think they were talking in a different language…but I wasn't close enough to hear what they were saying. So I walked up a little higher on the hill so I could see better. It seemed like the crowd spread out a little, and I could finally see what was going on."

"And what was it?"

Sophie's tears started again as she said, "There were three crosses with three men on them…and then I knew where I was!"

"Oh, Sophie," replied her mom, "that would have been very hard to see."

"It was! At first, I was really frightened. I was too far away to see everything, but I knew it was Jesus in the middle. He was different, somehow, though I'm not sure I can explain it. I could tell He was in a lot of pain, but it was…I don't know…kind of like a *quiet* or *still* pain—like maybe He knew what was going on and that it would soon be over."

"What happened then?"

"Well, it gets fuzzy then…you know how dreams are, but I just remember that somehow I wasn't frightened anymore, and I remembered the verse you gave me that is on my name poster—you know, about us being in Jesus, who became wisdom from God. You remember?"

"Yes," her mom said quietly.

"And I remember thinking that since Jesus became wisdom for us and died on the cross for us, maybe it's really important to learn all we can about what wisdom is. After that, I woke up, and I had tears running down my face. I was so sad…but it was a funny kind of sad…like…almost a *happy* kind of sad. Not happy like a 'fun party' happy, but more like something on the inside that felt like sunshine—like how it feels on a really cold day outside, and then you come inside where it's warm, and you're glad you're at home. But the tears surprised me, and they didn't stop, and I didn't know what to do about that, so I came in here."

"I'm glad you did. It *is* a surprising dream for someone your age, but it's one you will probably remember for the rest of your life. Do you think that maybe it was because we have been talking so much lately about wisdom and how it comes to us?"

"Maybe so," said Sophie. "There was another verse on my poster about looking for wisdom…something about searching for it…I can't remember it exactly. Do you?"

"I think it was, 'If you look for it as for silver and search for it as for hidden treasure, then you will understand the fear of the Lord and find the knowledge of God,'" replied her mom.

"So…wisdom is really about knowing Jesus, His Father, and the Holy Spirit."

"Yes, that's what it's all about."

"That kind of means that He knows everything, doesn't it?"

"Yes, Sophie, it does."

"Remember last week when you wrapped us up in the afghan and said that the afghan was like all the truth we knew about Jesus and that His truth was holding us?"

"I remember," said her mom.

"And that truth means that He really, really does love us, doesn't He?

"Yes, He really, really does love us!"

"And," Sophie continued, "He will help me every day, so I can try to live like Him?"

"Yes, He absolutely will!" replied her mom.

"Wisdom is hard to understand, Mom, but maybe it's just all about trying to live like Jesus. Our memory verse for this week is about watching over our hearts; it kind of means the same thing, doesn't it?"

"Yes, it does," said her mom, "and I think you have described it very well. If we live like Jesus, He will show us all the treasures of wisdom."

"Treasures?"

"Yes, *treasures!*" replied her mom.

"Hmmm…" Sophie yawned and then said, "My tears are gone now, but I think I want to thank Jesus for giving me this dream. Will you listen to me?"

"Absolutely," replied her mom.

"Dear Jesus, thank You for giving me this dream. Will You help me keep my heart so I can learn more about You and learn more and more about wisdom? But I'm really sleepy now, so I think I'll wonder about all of the *treasures* tomorrow. Amen."

Sophie paused for just a moment and said, "Is it all right if I sleep in here? It won't be long until morning. I'm so glad yesterday was Friday, so we don't have to get up early for school or work!"

"I am too, and yes, you may sleep in here."

"Thanks, Mom…I love you…goodnight."

"Goodnight, dear Sophie."

Sophie sighed and went to sleep immediately. And this time, it was her mother who lay quietly with tears streaming down her face as she thanked the Lord for His wonderful grace and for His wonderful little girl, Sophie.

* * *

As the sunlight peeked its way through the blinds and curtains the next morning, Sophie slowly awakened and, for a moment, was startled that she was not in her own bed. And then she remembered her dream and coming to her mom's room. As she lay there thinking about her dream, she wondered and wondered about it. *It was such a strange place*, she thought, *and the people were dressed so funny, and the language they spoke was so different.* But mostly, she wondered about Jesus. *I know He died*, she thought, *but I also know He came back to life in three days. That's what Easter is all about. He lived again, and…Oh yes, He still lives. I must go tell Mom that that is such a wonderful thing to wonder about.*

And Sophie jumped out of bed and went downstairs to share her wonder with her Mom!

Memory Verse: "Above all else, guard your heart, for everything you do flows from it" (Proverbs 4:23, NIV).

What Do You Think?

1. Do you dream often? Do you sometimes have dreams that are a little scary? Are you surprised that Sophie would dream about Jesus at the cross?
2. What do you think of Sophie's dream? Is it scary to you, or do you think it might be one that she will remember for a long time and be a blessing to her?

Prayer

Review Memory Verse: "Above all else, guard your heart, for everything you do flows from it" (Proverbs 4:23, NIV).

SUPPLY LIST FOR ACTIVITY 10

- Supplies to make the tree: brown paper
- One poster board for the tree
- Supplies for apples and leaves: red & green construction paper

* * *

Activity 10: Apples of Wisdom

Every chapter in *Life with Sophie* has had a memory verse for your child or children to learn. The activity for this last chapter is designed to bring to mind and have a symbol of each memory verse to be kept in their room, family room, or kitchen. Even though the poster will eventually come down, it is designed as a standing reminder of those verses and to aid them in remembering them until they are firmly established in their memory.

The purpose of the tree is to have a useful tool to help the children firmly plant these verses from Proverbs to memory. I have put in "Chapter Reminders" to help you remember the main events and the memory verse of each chapter.

As you put each apple on the tree, spend some time helping the children remember some of the events of Sophie, Sophie's family, and Sophie's friends as they lived day by day and began to see the reasons for obtaining wisdom.

Once again, it has been my great privilege to be a part of helping your children see the majesty of our God and His sovereign work in the lives of His children and His everlasting faithfulness to their individual worth and design for their lives.

Chapter Reminders

Chapter One: I Wonder

Sophie wonders about her name and why she was named Sophie. In finding out her name means wisdom, the conversation then goes to the meaning of wisdom and to the memory verse, "The fear of the Lord is the beginning of wisdom, and knowledge of the Holy One is understanding" (Proverbs 9:10, NIV).

Chapter Two: Treasuring a Good Name

Sophie's thoughts about her sister and how important our names are, not only for ourselves but also for the people who know us. They will have pleasant or unpleasant memories, which are understood by the memory verse, "A good name is more desirable than great riches; to be esteemed is better than silver or gold" (Proverbs 22:1, NIV). Also, this chapter introduces the uncertainty and fear that Sophie still has over the divorce of her parents.

Chapter Three: A Trusting Heart

Sophie's mom finds Sophie discouraged and afraid over her school lessons. Sophie's feelings can often be understood by children when they feel pressured to measure themselves by others. Remind them how precious they are and that this memory verse is for every child of God. "Trust in the Lord with all your heart and lean not on your own understanding; in all your ways submit to Him, and He will make your paths straight" (Proverbs 3:5–6, NIV).

Chapter Four: Sophie Speaks about Good Friends

Sophie's thoughts about her special friend and cousin, Jackson, the fun they have together as well as the relationship of trust they have established. Also, the devotionals for this chapter really emphasize the necessity of being a good friend as well as having good friends. This chapter's memory verse was, "Oil and perfume make the heart glad, and a person's advice is sweet to his friend" (Proverbs 27:9, NASB).

Chapter Five: The Deep and Terrible Woods

Sophie and Jackson are influenced by their friends to go into a forbidden part of the woods. After a big scare, Sophie tells them, "We should never have done this…" The memory verse is a good caution and sort of a pun on their experience. "Ponder the path of your feet; then all your ways will be sure" (Proverbs 4:26, ESV).

Chapter Six: The Deep and Terrible Trouble

Sophie and Jackson face the consequences of having disobeyed and find the consequences are hard. However, both of them are sorry for having been influenced to disobey and want to be stronger in their next temptation. The memory verse substantiates their thoughts. "My son, do not forget my teaching, but keep my commands in your heart, for they will prolong your life many years and bring you peace and prosperity" (Proverbs 3:1–2, NIV).

Chapter Seven: Lies and Ugly Words

Sophie is lied to by her friend and struggles with anger and great sadness. Her mom gently leads her to understand how to forgive and assures her that the Lord is with her and will help her. The memory verse especially helps her with the promise, "Do not say, 'I will repay evil'; wait for the Lord, and He will deliver you" (Proverbs 20:22, ESV).

Chapter Eight: Forgiveness and Grace

Sophie sees the power of forgiveness through the story of Jazelle from Africa. She also gets a call from her friend, who lied to her, and understands that the Lord really did do what He said He would. She can see that "He holds success in store for the upright; He is a shield to those whose walk is blameless" (Proverbs 2:7, NIV).

Chapter Nine: A Shelter in the Storm.

Sophie talks to her Uncle Mike about her parents' divorce and her struggles because she so misses her dad. Uncle Mike wisely shares the story of Joseph and that God will be faithful to use all her sorrows for her good and His glory. He is her defense and a strong tower, "The name of the Lord is a fortified tower; the righteous run to it and are safe" (Proverbs 18:10, NIV).

Chapter Ten: Sophie's Dream

Sophie's dream, though hard to see, helps her to see that truly all wisdom is found in Jesus, and we will find wisdom also as we are in relationship with Jesus, His Father, and the Holy Spirit. "Above all else, guard your heart, for everything you do flows from it" (Proverbs 4:23, NIV).

Instructions for the Wisdom of Apples Tree

Supplies:

- One white poster board, one brown postal paper,
- Three or four sheets of red construction paper (8.5 x 11) for the apples
- Five sheets of green construction paper (8.5 x 11) for tree foliage and extra leaves
- Memory verses of each chapter printed on white circles of paper to paste onto red apples
- One small container of Elmer's school glue

Directions:

1. The poster can be easily drawn as a pattern to follow by using the picture of the "Apples of Wisdom" picture that you see on the first page of Chapter 10. The tree trunk is simply two curves on the brown postal paper in the shape of the trunk and pasted on the white poster board. When using school glue, it often looks somewhat lumpy even though you flatten it out. But when it dries, it lies flat.
2. Using four sheets of green construction paper, make a rectangle and paste the sheets together in the form of a rectangle. Then, hand draw a puffy tree top similar to the picture. Cut the tree top out and paste it onto the tree trunk.
3. Using the stencil, draw ten apples on the red construction paper and cut those out.

4. Using the stencil, make ten circles on white paper and cut them out.
5. The verses are then cut out and pasted onto the circles. The circles are pasted onto the apples and then pasted onto the tree.
6. The leaves are cut out and pasted as if falling from the tree and on the ground.

7.

Scriptures for Apple	
Chapter 1	Chapter 2
"The fear of the Lord is the beginning of wisdom, and knowledge of the Holy One is understanding" (Proverbs 9:10, NIV).	"A good name is more desirable than great riches; to be esteemed is better than silver or gold" (Proverbs 22:1, NIV).
Chapter 3	Chapter 4
"Trust in the Lord with all your heart and lean not on your own understanding. In all your ways submit to Him and He will make your paths straight" (Proverbs 3:5–6, NIV).	"Oil and perfume make the heart glad, and a person's advice is sweet to his friend" (Proverbs 27:9, NASB).

Chapter 5	Chapter 6
"Ponder the path of your feet; then all your ways will be sure" (Proverbs 4:26, ESV).	"My son, do not forget my commands in your heart for they will prolong your life many years and bring you peace and prosperity" (Proverbs 3:1–2, NIV).
Chapter 7	Chapter 8
"Do not say 'I will repay evil'; wait on the Lord, and He will deliver you" (Proverbs 20:22, ESV).	"He holds success in store for the upright; He is a shield to those whose walk is blameless" (Proverbs 2:7, NIV).
Chapter 9	Chapter 10
"The name of the Lord is a fortified tower; the righteous run into it and are safe" (Proverbs 18:10, NIV).	"Above all else guard your heart, for everything you do flows from it" (Proverbs 4:23, NIV).

Apple Template for Tree
Size 3" x 3"

Endnotes

1   *The story of the stolen bike is adapted from Maranatha, posted on February 4, 2009.

CPSIA information can be obtained
at www.ICGtesting.com
Printed in the USA
BVHW051253220323
660917BV00004B/125